THE
DEVIL'S
ADVOCATE

100
BUSINESS RULES
YOU MUST BREAK

CASPIAN WOODS

Harlow, Englan   Sydney
Auckland •   w Delhi
Cape Town •   s • Milan

PEARSON EDUCATION LIMITED
Edinburgh Gate
Harlow CM20 2JE
United Kingdom
Tel: +44 (0)1279 623623
Fax: +44 (0)1279 431059
Web: www.pearson.com/uk

First published 2013 (print and electronic)

The right of Caspian Woods to be identified as author of this work has been asserted by him in accordance with the Copyright, Designs and Patents Act 1988.

Pearson Education is not responsible for the content of third-party internet sites.

ISBN: 978-0-273-77949-0   (print)
        978-0-273-78161-3   (PDF)
        978-0-273-78164-6   (ePub)

British Library Cataloguing-in-Publication Data
A catalogue record for the print edition is available from the British Library

Library of Congress Cataloging-in-Publication Data
A catalog record for the print edition is available from the Library of Congress

10 9 8 7 6 5 4 3 2 1
16 15 14 13 12

Cover design by Nick Redeyoff
Text design by Design Deluxe
Print edition typeset in 10/13.5pt Caslon book by 30
Print edition printed and bound in Great Britain by Henry Ling Ltd, Dorchester, Dorset

NOTE THAT ANY PAGE CROSS REFERENCES REFER TO THE PRINT EDITION

To Mr Coombes,

my third form English teacher who, in the lesson where he had the

class climbing all over the school desks barking like crazed hyenas,

taught me that 'convention' is only for the lazy and timid.

Contents

Part one
Leadership

Part two
Strategy

Part three
Innovation

Part four
Sales and marketing

Part five
Staff

Part six
Finance

Part seven
Personal

Author biography

If you learn more from failure than success, then **Caspian Woods** is at PhD standard.

He launched his first business producing student yearbooks, but decided to sell out a year before Facebook showed how it was possible to make billions from the same market. He launched his next business, an e-commerce magazine, by living for a week in a shop window, about six months before the dot com boom turned to bust. He then focused the business in financial marketing, working with Bank of Scotland and RBS...well, you get the picture.

Happily the business, Editions Financial, is still going strong and helps some of the world's largest companies devise content marketing strategies. Along the way, he's written a number of business books, and served as an Ambassador for the Prince's Trust, and they seem to have survived his advice.

Acknowledgements

My great thanks and undying appreciation to Julie Newing for her indefatigable work in digging up background research, making suggestions and fact-checking for this text.

To Stuart Martin for all his design support.

To Ruth, and all my colleagues at Editions Financial, for making coming to work so much fun. And also our clients for allowing us to get away with it for so long.

To my family and siblings, who got me over a fear of public ridicule by strapping me to a gatepost with a 'Do not feed the animal' sign.

Elie, Rachael, Sarah, Paul and the team at Pearson, for making the publishing process such a joy.

And to Scarlett and Felix for inspiring me, but no, you can't have a dog.

Publisher's acknowledgements

We are grateful to the following for permission to reproduce copyright material:

Profile of zebra © Digital Zoo/Corbis; Wooden puzzle cubes © Ocean/Corbis; Male karate black belt © JGI/Tom Grill/Blend Images/Corbis; Harley Davidson motorcycle © Car Culture/Corbis; Ants on a white background © Jan Bengtsson/Etsa/Corbis; Origami boat © Iris Friedrich/fstop/ Corbis; Numbers on running track © RG Images/Stock4B/ Corbis; Odd One Out © Kelly Redinger/Design Pics/Corbis;

Stacks of one pound coins © Image Source/Corbis; Hockey netting © Stephen Harrison/Alamy.

In some instances we have been unable to trace the owners of copyright material, and we would appreciate any information that would enable us to do so.

Introduction

This book does not have the answers. It will not make you a millionaire. It will not get you laid.

That's because, in truth, there are no simple answers. If the rules of success were that simple they could be copied out like a cookbook. There would be a serious shortage of business authors and we'd all be sitting in the Bahamas sipping Martinis instead!

While a particular lesson might have delivered a profit in the past, there's no guarantee it will in the future. In economic theory, profit is a signal to others to move into an industry and copy like crazy until the excess profits evaporate. Any company that manages to make huge profits, doing the same thing year in, year out, is not evidence of genius. It's evidence of a broken market.

But some businesses stay ahead of the pack. They don't do this by slavishly following a set textbook, but by adhering to a set of deeper principles. They think ahead, they zig when others zag, they quietly spot the opportunities that the frenzied herd has just galloped past.

The aim of this book is to cultivate that instinct. I hope it sharpens your maverick mind, and bolsters your gut instincts.

And if you are already the person who can stand apart, then I hope it provides more strength to your arm.

THEY ZIG WHEN

OTHERS ZAG,

THEY QUIETLY SPOT THE

OPPORTUNITIES

THAT THE FRENZIED

HERD HAS JUST

GALLOPED PAST.

Part one
Leadership

1
The only thing you need to be a great leader

"If you want to build a ship, don't drum up the men to gather wood, divide the work and give orders. Instead, teach them to yearn for the vast and endless sea."

– Antoine de Saint-Exupéry, *The Wisdom of the Sands*

There's more nonsense talked about 'leadership' than almost any other topic. I think it says more about consultants tapping into the loneliness of leaders, and their access to juicy budgets.

Leadership is simple. If you want people to follow you, you need to be going somewhere. And then you need to convince them that they want to come with you.

Researchers into the 'science' of happiness found one of the greatest contributors to well-being is a sense of purpose. In researching lottery winners, they found three main factors contributing to happiness; an absence of worry, closeness to family/friends and a sense of purpose (ironically, winning the lottery tended to remove all three).

Work is one of a few places people can define a sense of purpose. Your job as a leader is to describe the mountaintop to them, and why it's a great place to get to. Tell them about the challenges and ravines on the journey, and if there's an adversary trying to beat you there, then so much the better.

It'll get you more places than any amount of corporate paint-balling sessions ever will.

Action points

- Make sure you have a big, hairy, audacious goal in your business.
- Invest time in selling that vision to your team, and why they should join you in it.
- Let them know who the enemy is.

2
Ask for favours

I remember the poster on the wall of my primary school: 'Do unto others as you would have them do unto you.' As you grow up, you learn that if you want others to help you, you need to help them first. In business, this is expressed as building up a bank of 'social capital' that you can cash in when you really need it.

Well, I'm sorry, Mum and Dad, but it doesn't work that way. If you want someone's support, you need to ask *them* to do you a favour first.

It was Benjamin Franklin who first discovered this effect. To win a crucial vote, Franklin had to secure the backing of a rival senator. Finding that his rival had a passion for literature, Franklin pulled his masterstroke. Cornering him in the Senate library, he asked his rival to lend him a particularly valuable book of his, and then thanked him profusely. It worked a treat, and the senator went on to become a lifelong supporter. As Franklin observed: 'He that has once done you a kindness will be more ready to do you another than he whom you yourself have obliged.'

One reason for this effect, backed up by researchers, could be that favours create obligation. People like being in credit to you and not in debt. An extreme example is in Japan, where it's said you should not stop to help someone

who's fallen in the street as you will be placing on them an
unbearable obligation of debt.

Action point

- If you want someone to feel happy, put them in a
  position of power. Build a bond by asking them to help
  you out.

3
Sleep in your car

Companies spend eye-watering amounts of money on employee communications, trying 'to align behaviours with corporate values', and 'live the corporate vision'.

But we're not idiots. Like Soviet propaganda, we instantly discount anything we are told we should think. What we believe is what we see and experience with our own eyes.

So, if you are a leader, and want a message to be believed, don't lecture your staff. Do something epic that will be remembered. Stories are more powerful than any HR diktat.

Despite having a personal worth estimated at around £15 billion, Ikea founder Ingvar Kamprad is passionate that the culture of frugality is embraced throughout his corporation. So he drives around in an old Volvo, flies economy, and lives in a house furnished with Ikea furniture... which he assembled himself (he must be a whizz with an Allen key by now).

One night, visiting a new site with his team, he was frustrated that the local motels and B&Bs were charging what he saw as too much. So, despite the outside temperature being 15 degrees below freezing, he decided to sleep in the back of his car and insisted his managers did too (in their own cars, obviously).

Action points

- Decide what values you want to stand for.
- Think of a powerful way to embody this and go out and do it. If you don't 'live your values', you can hardly expect others to.

DO SOMETHING EPIC

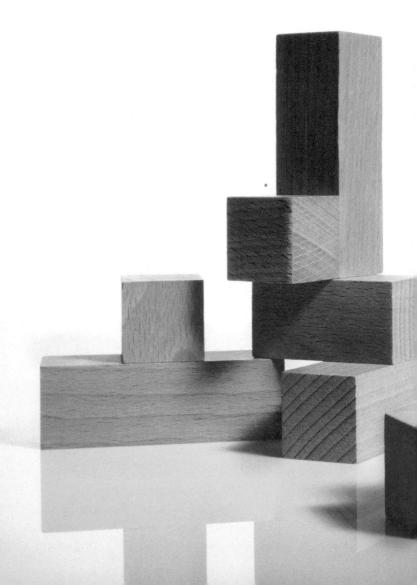

THAT WILL BE

REMEMBERED.

4

Leave stuff half-finished

My father once gave me a sage piece of advice: 'The best is the enemy of the good.' Although at the time I nodded to hide the fact I didn't understand, over time, it has sunk in.

The last 20 per cent of any job is the bit that takes the greatest effort. And life is a zero-sum game; any precious hours you spend doing one task are taken from what else you could be doing.

I'm not saying you can deliver a shoddy service. If someone doesn't see a job through, you'll fail fast. But that doesn't mean you have to be the one to finish it. If you spend 80 per cent of your time finishing things off, that's a hell of a lot of doors you won't have time to knock on.

On Belbin personality tests, one of the most rigid personality types is the 'completer-finisher'. They love the detail and tying up the loose ends. You need one in your team. But if you aren't one, then there is absolutely no point trying to become one. You'll probably cock it up, annoy all your co-workers and make yourself miserable.

Action points

- Our basic personality types are more fixed than we might care to think. When building a team, make sure you have the right personalities in the right roles.

- But if your goal is to drive your way to riches and glory, then accept you are going to have to let go of the steering wheel occasionally.

5
This software can kill you

There is a piece of software on your computer that has the potential to shorten your life, not to mention impact on your quality of work life.

It's your email. Turn it off.

You're beavering away on an important proposal and suddenly, 'Ping!', a message flashes up. 'Urgent', it says, before you read it to find you're cc'd on the inter-office car parking rota. You go back to your proposal, but you've lost your train of thought.

Sure, it's annoying, but where's the danger?

In a joint research exercise, the University of California and the US Military wired up a group of office workers to an EEG machine to monitor the effect email was having on them. Those in the group that had emails downloading automatically were found to have consistently higher heart rates than colleagues who turned off their email. This is the 'fight or flight' reaction that triggers the release of the stress hormone cortisol and leads to a higher risk of heart attacks and a range of health problems.

But it's also just a bad way to work. 'Urgent' and 'important' are not the same thing. By constantly allowing your agenda to be hijacked by messages that flag themselves as urgent, you'll never be able to focus on the important but less pressing matters.

I've seen the same approach trialled with physical interruptions. An ambitious exec convinced his company to issue little red and green flags for workers to put above their computers to indicate whether they were interruptible. A fine idea, until he walked in to work the next day to find *every* desk in the office had the red flag raised.

Action points

- Change your email settings so messages don't automatically download. Don't fret; if it's really urgent, the person will call you.
- Set aside a couple of specific times each day to check on emails and cover anything that's desperate.
- If you want to stop interruptions, don a pair of earphones. It's simple but makes people think twice before interrupting (apologies to all my colleagues!).

6
Forgive
(but don't forget)

Stuff happens.

At some stage in your business life, whatever your best endeavours, mistakes will hit you. And when they do, the temptation is to launch a witch-hunt. In your pain, you want to find the person responsible and give them grief.

It might make you feel better. It might give you a misguided sense that you've stopped it happening again, but you're very wrong. Instead, you're creating a culture of fear. Before long, people will start to cover up their mistakes. They'll shift blame and backstab. And then the cock-ups will come thick and fast.

As Arsenal Football Club manager Arsene Wenger says, 'You need to play without fear'. To stop things going wrong, take a safety lesson from the airline industry.

On an approach to Dulles International Airport in 1976, the pilot of TWA Flight 514 misunderstood an ambiguous response from air traffic control. In the subsequent crash, all 85 passengers and seven crew perished. On investigation, it turned out that this error had happened before, but those concerned had covered it up.

In response, the industry set up the Aviation Safety Reporting System. It's a confidential service where anyone in the industry at any level or rank is encouraged to report close calls or mistakes without fear of regulatory action against them. Since introducing this system, the rate of fatal accidents in their airline industry has dropped 65 per cent.

Action points

- When something goes wrong, set up an open debrief. It should be clear that there is no rank, there will be no records, and there will be no recriminations.

- Start by admitting your own deficiencies to get a clear and frank discussion.

- But at the same time, don't forget – you cannot make the same mistake twice.

7

Ignore urgent tasks

I f there's one business book I'd recommend, it's *The E-Myth* by Michael Gerber. As you're pushed for time, I'll save you some of the effort.

Gerber's main message is that you must spend more time working *on* your business, and less time *in* your business. You need to get out of the engine room and on to the bridge to see where the ship is going.

Many businesses I see are zombies. They're not insolvent, but they're not growing. They're stuck in a limbo land. And the reason they fail to grow is because they are run by technical experts or craftspeople who love delivering the actual product.

In order to grow, you need to build the systems and processes that mean anyone can deliver. As Gerber says, you need to look at the business as if it were a franchise.

To make this switch, you need to change how you spend and value your time. In particular, you need to focus on those tasks which don't seem urgent or pressing, but have the greatest impact on your long-term plans. As you probably don't have lots of spare time just kicking around, you free up this 'strategic' time by ignoring 'urgent' tasks which will have little long-term impact on your business.

It can be extremely hard to ignore a screaming child, but sometimes it's in their long-term best interests that you do so.

Action points

- Start a company manual that documents the systems that you need to get things done.

- Aim to make yourself redundant in any role you deliver, and do the same for your team.

- When writing a to-do list, try giving each item a score, based on long-term monetary impact and amount of effort. Get into the habit of focusing on those tasks with greatest impact for lowest effort (yes, picking up the phone to prospective clients!).

8
Be ill-informed

We live in a world of 24-hour, rolling news. National newspapers are dead in the water as they're too slow. People crave their news fix instantly through the internet, mobile, Twitter and TV.

But do we really need so much news? Sure we're worried about bombings in the Middle East, or currency crises in Europe, but does your success depend on your ability to know exactly what's going on in the world?

The trouble with too much news is not just that it's a waste of time; it's actively damaging.

One of the legendary rules of news is that 'if it bleeds, it leads'. Experimenters at McGill University found that people showed a greater physiological reaction to bad news, through brain activity and sweating. Sadly, good news is often just not 'news' in that sense and so goes ignored.

But as you gorge yourself on a never-ending diet of this negativity, it can have a corrosive effect on your well-being and on your performance.

A number of studies have looked at the 'recession index' – the correlation between consumer confidence and use of negative language in newspapers. But one surprising study looked at the direction of this relationship.

Researchers scored the language used in newspapers read by commuters into New York's financial district, and share price movement. They found a link between the two, but the surprising thing was the direction. Downward share movements didn't just result in negative coverage the following day, it was the other way round. Negative news in the morning *led* to price drops that day. A daily diet of negativity becomes a self-fulfilling prophecy.

Bad news is addictive, and disconnecting yourself from it can be scary. But there is little we can do about the scary world, and endlessly reading about it feeds a sense of powerlessness, and will start to corrode your motivations and judgements.

Action points

- Put yourself on a news diet. Change your browser homepage from BBC News. Don't wake up to the *Today* programme. Don't watch the 10 o'clock news at bedtime. Buy a box set instead.

- If your job requires you to stay connected, then try to limit yourself to industry updates and weekly or monthly news reviews. But ignore the news.

- Set up alerts on Google to keep you up to date with those things that are necessary then you can ignore the rest.

9
Use guilt to motivate

I bet there are times you wish you could replace your colleagues with robots. You know the systems that make the business run smoothly – the impossible bit is getting your team to stick to them. Whether it's completing time-sheets or putting the loo seat down, it seems like a depressing slog to keep nagging them to do what you know is right for them.

So one day, you decide to 'get biblical' on the problem. Rather than endlessly chastising, you put in a financial penalty for non-compliance.

Satisfying as it might be, you could find out that by formalising the sanction, you've suddenly made compliance even *less* likely.

Social scientists have long highlighted the power of hidden social rules that make societies stick together. Now economists have shown their monetary value.

A team in Israel set out to change parents' behaviours around childcare. To dissuade parents from being late to pick up their children from day-care centres, they introduced a financial penalty. Every time a parent was late, they would be fined. But instead of cutting the number of late pick-ups, it *doubled* the rate. All of a sudden, they were sending out a signal that it was socially OK to be late, you just had to pay a premium for the service. The financial price bothered parents far less than the social price of the cross faces and silent stares of staff as they slunk in five minutes late.

Action points

- Think twice before formalising penalties and rewards for good and bad behaviour. Not only do you risk people 'gaming' the system, you remove the most painful sanction.
- Look instead for the equivalent of a 'naughty step'. OK, you might not go as far as the company that made trainees wear a cabbage on their heads, but the simple act of listing someone's name in the weekly meeting minutes can have a far more powerful effect.

10
Say less

11

Wait for the tide to go out

I t's hard not to feel like a Luddite. I read in the newspaper that Instagram has been bought for $1 billion. I see companies taking on legions of staff despite having no discernible source of revenue. And all the time, the industry trendsetters chastise me for not 'getting it', or understanding that 'this time, the rules have changed'.

So do you have the guts to sit the dance out, while everyone makes shedloads of money?

Sit on your hands. As the Sage of Omaha, Warren Buffett says, 'It's only when the tide goes out that you see who's been swimming without any trunks.'

Just as there is the 'wisdom of the crowd' there is also the stampede mentality of the herd. Hold close to your heart the dictum that 'If things look too good to be true, they probably are'. When everyone starts telling you to do something, it's probably time to head in the opposite direction. Legendary tycoon Joseph Kennedy summed this up when he said he knew to get out of the stock market just before the Wall Street Crash in 1929 when the boy shining his shoes started to give him share tips.

And if you 'don't get it', the risk is you'll jump on the bandwagon just as it is pulling out of the station. Look no further than old media hand Rupert Murdoch, who bought MySpace in 2005 for $580 million, only to sell it six years later for $35 million.

On the flip side, just because nobody gets your idea yet, or the world isn't quite ready, it's no time to give up.

Action points

- Trust your intuition. No matter how much others try to convince you, if it doesn't feel right, then it's not right for you.
- And don't be disheartened by an unappreciative public. They might just need a bit more warming up to come round to your ideas.

12
Ask the bride to dance

Have you ever noticed how supermodels seem to have surprisingly ugly boyfriends?

This came to mind at a wedding as I watched the bride sit on her own watching the dancing. She was the object on the pedestal, and no one thought to go up and ask if she'd actually like a dance. It's the same with the beautiful girl at your school. It's often the guy with the most chutzpah and least to lose that has the courage to not take them seriously and make fun of them.

It's the same in business. I recently watched an entrepreneur at a dinner go up and tap the Chief Executive of Sainsbury's on his shoulder and have a chat about why they must stock his product. He was polite and quick, but he certainly didn't pussyfoot around like the rest of us worrying that 'it wasn't the done thing'. (Though to this day, I do regret trying to shake hands with Richard Branson just as he was zipping up in the men's toilets at an awards dinner.)

Action points

- There will be a number of individuals who have the insight or clout to transform your business or career. Work out who they are, what you need to know, then approach them.
- Treat it like a first date; don't get all formal and expect a huge commitment from them. Just make the best use of your time and theirs by doing your homework and being incredibly focused on what you need to know. They'll value that.

13
Take fewer risks

One of the basic tenets of economics holds that profit is the reward for risk. You can see it most visibly in finance with the risk and reward ratios for investing in asset classes like shares and bonds (theoretically!).

But try asking a mountain climber or freefall parachutist if they like to take risks. Mountaineer Sir Chris Bonnington holds close to his mother's dictum, 'Do dangerous things safely'. Or as Chief Scout, adventurer and all-round hero of small boys, Bear Grylls had drilled into him by his father, 'If there's any doubt, there's no doubt'. People setting out on these amazing adventures go to considerable lengths to remove as many risks as they possibly can.

It might be machismo, it might be laziness, but there is no need to take unnecessary risks in business.

To succeed, you need to set out on the path less trodden, and make a reach no one else has. But you'd be a fool not to do all in your power to protect your downsides, whether through insurance, back-up plans or fail-safes.

But once you've thought it through, file your insurances in the bottom drawer, or in the back of your mind. You can't let doubt hinder you. As the German philosopher Goethe urged: 'Once you commit, then providence moves. Whatever you can do, or dream you can do, begin it. Boldness has genius, power and magic to it.'

Action points

- Do a risk MOT or audit in your business. Write down all the obvious, and even less obvious risks the business might face.

- Then go through the list and think of a remedy for each. You don't have to sort all the risks immediately, but even the awareness that comes from thinking them through can help you avoid them.

Part two
Strategy

14
Don't diversify

Nobody wants all their eggs in one basket. It makes sense to spread your risk by widening your product range and diversifying into related markets. Besides, if you've got a happy customer in your hot little hands, then you want to sell them lots of other things too.

But what is it they say about the 'Jack of all trades'?

As humans, we have a bias against 'goal dilution'. While researching motivation, behavioural scientist Ayelet Fischbach at the University of Chicago conducted experiments which showed that by adding more goals to an activity (e.g. 'exercise to build muscle *and* lose weight'), the less likely people were to undertake the activity.

And as consumers, we evaluate offerings the same way. Just think of your local Starbucks. You might be happy going there for coffee. But would they be your first choice for fresh sandwiches?

Or have you ever been sneered at when picking a combined hi-fi system by music cognoscenti who say you only get quality from hi-fi separates?

Besides, German companies the world over have proved that picking a small niche market is no barrier to growing a world-class enterprise (more on this in Rule 21: Don't dance where elephants play).

Action points

- You don't want your coffee-shop customers going hungry, but beware that the more you promote diverse offers, the more you will weaken customer perceptions of your core competence.

- If your worry is risk, look for lateral ways to diversify. Explore routes to take your exact same specialism into tangential markets without weakening it.

15
Stop obsessing about quality

Are you a victim of Total Quality Management? Been battered by ISO Standards? Sick of Six Sigma?

It appears that the 'quality' business has been taken over by the pointy-headed, clipboard brigade. They exhibit a borderline obsessional urge to remove every vestige of error from the world, and leave it a calm, clear place of functional order.

So how come we lust after iPhones and not Sony mobiles?

While Apple notched up a huge $22 billion profit in 2011, Japan's largest gadget-makers revealed they expect to lose a combined $17 billion. Since 2000, Japan's consumer electronics giants have lost two-thirds of their market value.

And yet when it came out, was the iPhone more reliable than a Sony phone? As if! Apple had contrived to build the aerial into the body of the phone to the extent that if I hold the phone the wrong way, I can't make a call. In similar ways, I've got grazed wrists from the razor-sharp aluminium edges of my Mac laptop, and almost singed my bedsheet with the heat from its battery packs. But I'm drooling at the front of the queue when a new Apple product comes out.

I'm not saying you can tolerate a business that continually turns out shoddy and unreliable goods. But we must reclaim the term 'quality'. Quality is not an absence of errors. It is about magic, joy and beauty. We should strive to build products and services that make customers rock back in delight, not ones that simply 'deliver consistently'.

Action point

- Put the pointy-headed brigade back in their cages, and let slip the dogs of creative abandon.

16
Embrace awkward suppliers

ood suppliers are vital to your success. When your
back's against the wall and customers are pressur-
ing you to deliver, your reputation is at stake if you
don't have a supplier who's going to be there for you.

So when evaluating a new supplier, be suspicious of
anyone who is too positive.

Overeager salespeople will say anything to win a new customer. But when you've got a customer crying for delivery
and you phone your supplier, chances are the salesperson
will be sunning themselves on a Caribbean beach courtesy
of the fat commission cheque they earned from you.

But if you've got a supplier who's moaning, or asking
awkward questions about the kind of work you might give
them and complaining about delivery schedules, don't dis-
miss them as being too much hard work. That sharp intake
of breath and the nervous pen tapping means they're taking
you seriously. They're weighing up the cost of their own
reputation, and whether they can fulfil the promises you are
asking them to make. When the crunch point comes, they
are the ones who'll be there to deliver, because they're the
ones who genuinely care and keep their promises.

Action points

- When weighing up a new supplier, use the salesperson for introductions, but then bypass them.

- Get the name of the factory supervisor and then go and meet them in person. Nosey around the factory. Have a frank conversation about what you're expecting of them, and don't be upset if they don't soft-soap you.

17
Fight like Nelson

In the Age of Sail, naval battles were an attritional process. Each warship would line up against its opponent and open fire. Eventual victory would go to the ship that was 5 per cent faster at reloading, or marginally more accurate.

As a young commander, Vice Admiral Nelson had made a name for himself as a maverick. During the Battle of Copenhagen, when ordered to retreat by Admiral Parker, he reputedly lifted his telescope to his blind eye and claimed, 'I really do not see the signal.'

His defining battle was at Trafalgar. Facing the standard line of the opposing French fleet, Nelson resolved to abandon the standard rules of engagement. Rather than advancing on all fronts, he arranged his fleet into two lines. He drove this straight into the centre of the French fleet in a massive concentration of firepower. It divided the French fleet, and delivered Nelson a stunning victory.

While not wanting to fall into trite 'business is war' analogies, there is a powerful lesson here.

While it's a concentration of firepower that will deliver victory, too often businesses hamstring themselves by advancing on all fronts. The most important decision you can often make is what you *won't* do.

There are competing demands in business, and pressure to do them all. But your resources, be they cash, manpower, or your own thinking time, are finite.

You need to decide first what will deliver your killer blow in business. Then rule out everything else, and advance only in a single line.

Action points

- What would deliver a decisive competitive advantage in your industry?

- Work out the actions, and dependencies, that will deliver this victory.

- Then go through your plan and delete any job or task that will not contribute directly to this victory. And whenever faced with a new task, put it to this test.

18
Your next competitor makes toilet paper

Got a good idea who your competitors are? Chances are you glare at their table at industry shindigs. Their delivery drivers cut yours up at roundabouts. You've hopefully spent a fair bit of time mapping their strengths and weaknesses, and how you compare.

But they're not the ones you should worry about.

Nokia are one of the world's leading mobile phone companies. Yet 20 years ago, before they'd ever set sight on a mobile, they were still a world leader – only in toilet paper manufacturing.

And for the first decade of this millennium, UK newspapers embarked on a ferocious price war to win market share from each other. Today their business model has been hollowed-out by San-Francisco resident Craig Newmark who, in setting-up Craigslist.com to keep in touch with his friends, heralded a devastating flight of classified advertising from the papers.

The greatest threats to your company are companies and business models of which you are only dimly aware. The exponential increase in the pace of innovation in business today means they will be stealing your lunch faster than ever.

Action points

- You need a network that is scanning for industry changes. It means not looking in the usual places, and is probably made up of people a good deal younger than yourself.

- Think laterally if there are other ways of delivering what you deliver.

- If someone isn't doing it, then do it yourselves. Because if you can think of it, then so can someone else, and your main competitive advantage is speed.

19

Burn your business plan

One of the first things you are told in business is to produce a business plan. Banks love 'em. It's hardly surprising; if you're asking them to take a bet on you – they want to know you've thought it through.

But believing that the next three years, let alone six months, can somehow be ordained by writing it down on a piece of paper is a fallacy best left to clairvoyants.

Instead you have to become a black belt in Miuayga, or 'Make it up as you go along'.

As Prussian general Helmuth von Moltke the Elder observed, 'No plan survives first contact with the enemy.' However, this wasn't a blanket rejection of planning. Indeed von Moltke was an eminent strategist. But he recognised that only the beginning of a campaign could be planned for. Thereafter it was a matter of adapting to 'the inevitable frictions of battle, chance events, imperfections in execution and the independent will of the opposition'. With his general staff, von Moltke worked through endless variations and adaptations, but then relied on the leadership instincts of the generals on the ground to adapt.

The problem with a business plan is that it doesn't do that. You invest a huge effort to fine-tune three-year forecasts and crunch the numbers, but then it sits in the bottom drawer.

In business, tactics are more important than strategy. You need a defining vision (perhaps written on the back of a napkin). But you then need to be quick and flexible about how you are going to get there.

Action points

- Sketch your vision on no more than a single piece of A4 paper.
- Replace your annual planning session with impromptu strategy 'mash-ups' where you run through possible opportunities and threats.
- Bring in a Devil's Advocate to challenge you.

BECOME A

BLACK BELT

IN MIUAYGA,

OR 'MAKE

IT UP AS YOU

GO ALONG'.

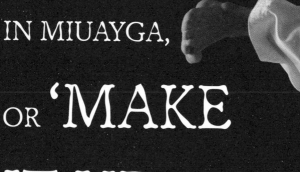

20
Set unrealistic goals

Ever been on a time management course and been badgered about SMART goals? Apparently, we should only have goals that are Specific, Measurable, Achievable, Realistic and Timed.

I've had to sit at the back of these classes gnawing my complimentary hotel pen to stop myself leaping up to seize control of the flip chart.

What's the point of having goals and dreams if they're realistic? If they were reasonable, 'achievable' or 'realistic' then they wouldn't be goals. The whole point of having audacious goals is that they seem unrealistic.

Was it realistic for a young, black, Jewish, poverty-stricken schoolgirl from the toughest housing project in Harlem to think she could win an Oscar? Tell that to Whoopi Goldberg.

Was it achievable for a single mother living off benefits in a rented flat to become Britain's wealthiest woman in ten years? JK Rowling managed it.

Was it realistic for a shy, young Indian lawyer to free a nation and change the world through non-violent civil disobedience? I'm glad Gandhi didn't believe that.

These people weren't realistic and they aren't constrained by limiting beliefs of what is achievable, or indeed measurable. How did Steve Jobs think he would measure his mission to 'put a ding in the universe'? Your reach must always exceed your grasp.

Action points

- Polish your dreams; nurture and feed them.
- Don't fret about how you'll get to the mountain-top, just obsess in detail about what you'll do in the next few days or weeks to move forwards.
- Put your faith in burning ambition, commitment and providence to take you there.

21
Don't dance where elephants play

For much of the last decade the prevailing model of Western capitalism has been the all-conquering, diversified conglomerate that uses its clout and connections to move from sector to sector. The model has been picked up by Indian titans like Tata, selling everything from Tetley tea bags to Jaguar cars.

But for the last 200 years, Germany's mid-market companies have been quietly sailing on a different tack. The 'Mittelstand' is the engine of German economic prosperity; a backbone of medium-sized, family-run and conservative companies that stick very resolutely to their niches. It might be wheels for hospital beds, lead pencils like Faber-Castell or train braking systems. But from Beijing to Basingstoke, look at the label, and chances are, you'll see a German name.

The Mittelstand share a number of characteristics that have been unfashionable of late.

They abhor debt, forsaking faster growth for complete control. They are often family-owned, and avoid outside shareholders. They have workers on their boards, and manage to keep their manufacturing operations in Germany.

And, vitally, they stick to their knitting. 'Don't dance where elephants play' is a favourite saying. They take a very small niche that has often been overlooked by larger multinationals. Then they set about dominating this niche globally, becoming virtual oligopolies and building 'defensive moats' that are hard for any competitor to assault.

Action points

- Dominate your niche. Keep a laser focus on what makes your product or service unique, and keep investing to maintain that leadership position.

- If you want to grow, don't diversify, but think global and take your niche to the world.

22
More IT is not the answer

'Ooh look, you can slide the icon with your fingers! Mmmm, I can pick the colour of the different screens!' I've sat in meetings where otherwise stony-hearted corporate executives have been morphed into excited toddlers by a whizzy technology demonstration.

Hats off to the IT sales guys, but it's made me realise I don't want to be the chump on the other side of the table.

The answer to most business problems is not more shiny technology. Having an integrated Customer Relationship Management system won't streamline your sales process. Scanning all your documents won't deliver the paperless office. Ten-foot-high teleconference screens won't give you the same benefits of a face-to-face meeting.

The NHS has just scrapped a computerised patient record system which cost £12.7 *billion*. Yet thousands of kilometres away, management consultants flock to Mumbai to watch the Dabbawallas in action. Each morning this tribe of delivery workers will collect 200,000 individual hot lunches in tiffin boxes. By 12.45, they will deliver these to the correct office desks, with each box on average changing hands four times, and travelling 60 km. Their error rate is one mistake every six million deliveries. There is not a single microchip in the process.

The problem with most technology solutions is the person sitting in front of the machine. It is their irrational behaviour that will govern how successful the project is. The success of the Dabbawallas is down to a village honour code that says 'Error is horror', a tight-knit tribal network and a passionate sense of pride.

If you want to streamline a process, start by changing behaviours. Once you've done that, then bring in the shiny kit. Shiny kit will not stop people being stupid, it will just equip them to do stupid things, only much faster.

Action points

- If you want your team to change behaviours, look at what drives their current actions. Then think what psychological factors would lead to better performance, whether it's pride or a vested interest in the outcome.

- Once you have this sorted, look at gradually streamlining the process with technology.

23

There's no prize for predicting the Flood

Good ideas are worthless.

You can spend all your life raving from the mountain-top about the future you can foretell. But the people who succeed are the ones who take action. Noah wasn't immortalised because he predicted the Flood. It was because he built the Ark.

In business, you need to stop fretting about creating the perfect product. An imperfect idea brilliantly executed is always better than a perfect one that limps to market. At the point that product meets market, there's always time to adjust and adapt. As an old banner at Apple's HQ read: 'Real artists ship.'

In his seminal management text, *In Search of Excellence*, Tom Peters identified the 'Bias to Action' as a defining trait in successful companies. As he quotes Herb Kelleher, legendary co-founder of low-cost US Southwest Airlines, as saying, 'Sure we have a strategic plan. It's called doing things.'

Even large companies can get with this. Consumer goods giant P&G have adopted what they call a 'testing fetish'. It means allowing staff members to fix problems on the spot, using their own initiative rather than relying on a top-down approach. It can mean short deadlines and a willingness to test solutions in a live environment.

Action points

- Measure success in your business by outputs, not by inputs. Focus on the results, not the effort.
- If your product is 80 per cent ready, it's ready. That remaining 20 per cent you can fix on the fly rather than back on the drawing board.

NOAH WASN'T

IMMORTALISED BECAUSE

HE PREDICTED THE

FLOOD.

IT WAS BECAUSE HE

BUILT THE

ARK.

24
Embrace chaos

As CEO of India's fastest growing retailer, Kishore Biyani was keen to learn what he could from Western management thinking. In expanding his Big Bazaar supermarkets, he emulated the look of Western supermarkets, installing bright lighting, neatly organised aisles, tidy and clean displays.

But he noticed that while customers could easily walk up and down the aisles, they then proceed to walk straight back out the door. So he broke up the displays with untidy aisles, and jumbled products together. He stopped selling polished apples, but left the fruit and vegetables with dirt and mud on them.

As he explains: 'You must keep Kama (creative spirit) and Yama (control) in proper balance in your firm.' In his effort to impose order, he'd made the shopping experience sterile, when what customers yearned for was the hustle and bustle that evoked the quality and freshness of a farmers' market. Customers were far more likely to pick up a product in a loose bag than disturb a neat stack.

Action points

- In an effort to impose calm and control in your business, have you over-engineered it to the point that working with you has become a sterile experience?

- Perhaps you need to let a bit of Kama loose on your organisation. It might be scary, but also more friendly and comfortable for customers to engage with you.

25
Sell invisibles

In the eyes of many traditionalists, if you don't make a physical product, then you're not a real business. What's the point of endless 'service businesses' if they've no one to service?

But times are changing. In the last ten years, the weight of a dollar's worth of US exports has halved. Today, 70 per cent of the value of a new car is intangible. As Jonas Ridderstråle and Kjell Nordström observed in *Funky Business*: 'If your competitive advantage hurts when you drop it on your foot, then you've got a problem.'

Whatever you sell, chances are that the greatest value you add is invisible.

Take the case of a German manufacturer recently cited in *The Economist* magazine. Looking round his vast factory, he told the interviewer: 'We don't sell refrigeration machines. We sell coldness.'

He's not suffering from a virulent outbreak of management bollockitis. He's demonstrating how companies are justifying a higher price by adding service to the mix. If you want to get technical, it's a 'hybrid value-added model'.

Closer to home, the flag carrier for UK manufacturing, Rolls Royce, now makes over half of its revenue not from selling engines, but from services that support that kit.

Much of the impetus for this change came from experiences in emerging economies. Companies found that entrepreneurial Chinese engineers could strip down a Western product, and rebuild a version for a fraction of the cost in a matter of weeks. Close them down and they'll open another factory across the street.

But if, like the German manufacturer, your contract isn't to supply '15 refrigerators', but 'to guarantee to maintain temperature at minus 26 degrees for 365 days a year', it's much harder to copy. Now your offering is about the quality of the machines, your after-sales servicing, support and consultancy. Your offering is much more tightly aligned to the interests of the customer, and your margins can be higher.

Action points

- What is the net benefit to the customer of your product and service?
- Working back from this point, think, 'What if I guaranteed to deliver a set amount of this value?'
- Then think about how you could structure the financial terms of this contract so your interests are aligned with those of your customer.

26

Use a lawyer like
a condom

"For refund, insert baby."

– Graffiti on condom vending machine

The best use of a lawyer is prophylactically, i.e. before you need them. If you are picking up the phone to one to sort out a problem, you are probably too late.

When you feel aggrieved or wronged by another party, it's tempting to come over all litigious. But heed the ancient Chinese maxim, 'When seeking revenge, dig two graves.'

The problem has already happened. While the rush to litigate might assuage your wounded sense of pride, chances are you'll just dig yourself into a bigger hole.

I knew of a software company who felt Microsoft had infringed one of their trademarks. In a David against Goliath display of business bravado, they took on the Seattle leviathan – and won! However, they'd spent so much time and attention on the legal battle that, despite a payout, the business had suffered to the extent it soon folded.

A good lawyer will tell you as much. We're lucky to work with a law firm who 'speak business'. They will first spell out the legal routes. Then they will talk through the likely business outcome and costs, and urge you to use common sense. I'm sure they are doing themselves out of fat fees in doing this, but it means I'll always pick up the phone for their advice.

Action points

- If your lawyer only speaks legalese, then ditch them.
- Do a legal fire drill. First explain your budget, then get your lawyers to have a look around the business and draw up a list of the largest risks, with priorities and an approximate cost for fixing them.

27
Target the poor

Over the next ten years, one billion people in emerging economies are set to enter the global middle class, in what will be the biggest period of wealth creation in history. Following the legendary dream of every Hong Kong entrepreneur 'to sell a toothbrush to every Chinaman', this is a market few should ignore.

However, the term 'middle class' is relative. In many countries you would qualify with a disposable income of just $4 a day.

This is forcing companies to think more creatively about how they package their products. For some, it's a 'sachet economy' where they shrink products to smaller sizes. Or follow Levi's in India who allow fashion-conscious but cash-strapped customers to rent their most desirable jeans. Or you can embrace the Indian concept of 'jugaad', a frugal methodology of 'making do with what you have', and strip products down to their bare essentials, as with the £1,000 Tata Nano car.

But isn't this exploiting these customers? Absolutely.

In his book, *The Fortune at the Bottom of the Pyramid,* the late Indian management guru, CK Prahalad, chided those who saw the only way to alleviate poverty as aid and not trade.

Companies like America's D-Rev exemplify this approach. As co-founder Dr Paul Polak expounds, 'The single most important thing the poor need to get out of poverty is to find a way to earn more money.'

Polak's company (mantra: 'Design for the other 90 per cent') sets out to develop products that will create new sources of income for the poor. The electro-chlorinator is a good example. Rather than a pricey water filtration system, it uses a solar panel and salt to produce a low-cost bleach. For a small investment, it allows a franchised water entrepreneur to treat water on their premises and sell 200 litres of water per hour.

Action points

- Are you blindly ignoring the biggest emerging consumer markets the world has ever seen?

- Could you empower your new customers to get rich off your back?

28

Don't make it in China

Over the last decade, the manufacturing sectors of many Western economies have been eviscerated by the rush to 'offshore' to low-cost centres like China and India.

But recently, there seems to be a subtle shift in this tide. Jobs are coming home.

Partly this is due to China overheating. Real wage costs have increased 40 per cent in a year in some regions, and fickle workers will shift jobs for the smallest incentive. I've spoken to manufacturers who dread the Chinese New Year holiday as many of their workers simply don't return afterwards. Compounding this are rising shipping costs and infrastructure hurdles (such as the 'one-week traffic jam' in one regional port), and concerns over rampant intellectual property theft. It makes purely financial calculations far trickier.

But there are other reasons to reconsider.

For some products, a 'Made in the UK' quality mark commands a price premium with customers. For fashion companies, the speed from catwalk to shop window is crucial (one Spanish retailer is jokingly said to make its clothes on the ships that deliver them). For others, there's a need to have their service and repair operations close at hand to their customers.

And Germany has managed to retain clusters of high-value manufacturers in its homeland, only relying on emerging countries for final assembly.

Technology is playing its part. Innovations in manufacturing technology are driving down the percentage labour costs in a product. And the rise of 3D printers and 'additive manufacturing' techniques make possible smaller-run customisation.

It may not turn into a flood, but rather than just looking at a basic labour cost, companies should view their manufacturing strategy by looking at a more balanced 'total cost' before packing their bags for China.

Action points

- If you are looking to offshore work to China, make sure your calculations factor in the total cost of doing business there.

- Also think carefully about the tangential benefits of keeping your production close to your customers.

Part three
Innovation

29
Reward failure

"Our greatest glory is not in never failing,
but in rising up every time we fail."

– Ralph Waldo Emerson

The popular image of the inventor is that of the mad scientist locked up in a tower, dreaming up the perfect product that they will unleash upon the world. In truth, it's a much more fragmented process. And at its heart lies failure.

'If you want to discover something that other people haven't,' says British inventor James Dyson, 'you need to do things the wrong way.' In designing his bagless vacuum cleaner, Dyson made 5,126 prototypes before he got it right. Understandably, this has made Dyson an advocate for the power of failure, saying: 'I've always thought schoolchildren should be rewarded for the number of failures they've had.'

The problem is that the opposite is the case and, from an early age, we are taught to shun failure as if it were somehow infectious, rather than a part of the natural process.

In your company, the solution could be to set up a 'lab' where you and your team can make these mistakes cheaply, quickly and capture the lessons from each one.

A great example is the one set up in Menlo Park, New Jersey, in 1876 by the then unknown inventor, Thomas

Edison. Under his guidance, a team of 60 collaborated on 40 different projects, working long hours and burning through countless mistakes. On his efforts to make the first commercially viable light bulb, Edison said, 'I have not failed 1,000 times. I have successfully discovered 1,000 ways to *not* make a light bulb.' In a six-year period, his team patented more than 400 inventions, including the light bulb and the phonograph.

Action points

- Don't mope over your failures or lock them in a dark cupboard. Pick them apart to find out exactly what when wrong, and put it right in your next attempt.

- Set up an 'innovation lab' in your business. It can be as simple as a process that allows you to quickly road-test each iteration of the new product before you take it to the market.

- If you haven't worked through at least ten failed prototypes of your new product or service, you're probably not ready yet.

30
Sacrifice the sacred cow

In the 1980s, Kodak enjoyed a 90 per cent share of the US film market and sales of $10 billion. Such was its dominance that 'a Kodak moment' entered common parlance as a memory to savour.

By 2012, it was bankrupt.

How could they have been so knuckle-headed they didn't spot the rise of digital cameras? In fact, they had. In 1975, Kodak's designers had produced one of the first digital cameras (with a resolution of 0.1 megapixels and weighing 3.6 kilograms!). Its boffins knew where the future lay. The problem was that its executives just couldn't accept it because they were making too much money from selling film.

It's a salutary lesson that the greatest barrier to creativity in established businesses is often the fear of what you stand to lose. Most companies fail to tack with the winds of change because in doing so, they'd have to sacrifice much of their existing revenue.

So it's no surprise that much groundbreaking innovation comes from new entrants to an industry. Gurus say this is because they're younger, more nimble, or better able to think creatively. In reality, it's mostly because they've got nothing to lose and everything to gain by making the change.

It takes brass cojones to make this change, but it's not impossible. IBM created the mainframe computer business, the minicomputer, and the personal computer business before selling out of each business and moving on to the next big thing.

If you're an incumbent, you must realise that just because you're making boatloads of cash at the moment, this doesn't give you a God-given licence to carry on printing money into the future.

Action points

- Accept that just because you choose not to embrace the future, a competitor won't come and take it from you.

- If needs be, set up a 'pirate business' outside your own, as your current company will want to stifle this new upstart (see Rule 80: Cultivate some enemies).

31
You are in the wrong business

When someone asks you at a party what business you are in, what do you say?

I'm guessing you'll give an obvious answer. Obvious, and wrong.

What business would you say Harley Davidson are in? The motorcycle business? The transportation industry? Nope, they're in the toy business.

When Harley Davidson analysed their customer base, they found their typical buyer was a 47-year-old man with an income of more than £50,000. When it came to asking why they'd bought a Harley, they weren't looking for a particularly effective way of getting in to work in the morning. They were rewarding themselves.

And when they analysed what the competition was for this 'lifestyle reward' spending, it wasn't other motorbikes. It was glass conservatories. In the US, it was swimming pools.

This isn't just a parlour game. If you truly understand what customers are buying from you – their deeper psychological needs or emotions – then you can radically enhance your pricing model, your marketing strategy and distribution. Parker Pens did this when they realised they were in the 'gift' business and not a pen company. They stopped competing against pen companies, but priced and advertised themselves against golf clubs – their closest competitor.

Action points

- Stop thinking what function your product or service delivers, and start asking: 'What is the greatest benefit our business offers to our customers?'

- Build out from this the deeper needs your business might fulfil for customers. Then look at who your real competitors are, and go after them.

WHAT BUSINESS WOULD YOU SAY...

THE MOTORCYCLE BUSINESS?

THE TRANSPORTATION INDUSTRY?

NOPE, THEY'RE IN THE...

... HARLEY DAVIDSON ARE IN?

...TOY
BUSINESS.

32
Sleep with your customers

How well do you know your customers? You know their ages, where they live, perhaps even what kind of car they drive. That's not enough. If you want to get ahead, you need to know what keeps them awake at 3 am; their hopes, desires and fears that even they would struggle to put into words.

To do this, some of the more forward-thinking companies around the world employ anthropologists. More traditionally to be found studying African or South American tribes, these naturally nosey researchers live as part of the community and literally walk in their sandals to truly understand them.

When applied to business, this approach can lead to penetrating insights.

P&G found women in poor Indian communities didn't necessarily want cheaper shampoo. Having the most lustrous hair is about finding a husband, and is therefore worth spending more money on. Nokia found customers in Asia shared their mobiles, so added shared address books, as well as torches to help in power cuts. Wondering why their washing machines were breaking down, Haier despatched a researcher who found some customers in rural China were also using their machines to wash potatoes. They responded by making the drums more robust.

And it works just as well closer to home. Some doctors' surgeries in the UK found that increasing the space to 'park' buggies led to fewer cancelled appointments as stressed mothers could bring all their kids in to an appointment.

Action points

- You need to know your customers' 3 am moments. By all means, ask them, but far better, try to shadow them for a day or two.

- Find out what makes them tick and what their main frustrations are with current products and services. By helping them sidestep these problems, you can come up with a 'killer app' for your business.

33

Judge the book by its cover

The traditional design process works something like this. The engineers invent a product, it goes to manufacturing, then design and finally, the marketing team get to do the fluffy packaging and promotion.

The trouble is that, as consumers, we're shallow creatures. When judging many products, we see the form as more important than the function.

Just ask the man voted by *Harvard Business Review* as the world's most successful CEO. Nope, not Mr Jobs, but Yun Jong-Yong. Under his helm, South Korea's Samsung increased its market capitalisation by $127 billion, a return of 1,458 per cent.

Jong-Yong did this by getting out of the commoditised 'me-too' chip manufacturing business, to focus Samsung on being a design-led business.

He sent his designers on sabbaticals to Italian fashion houses to watch and learn. Concerned that the traditional Korean Confucian management style of order and process would stifle creativity, he moved the design department away from the corporate HQ.

Most importantly, Jong-Yong turned Samsung's traditional product-development cycle on its head. The process now starts with designers; they'll dream up the box, then they go to the engineers to see if they can fill it.

He also instilled a relentless attention to the smallest detail. One of their sound engineers spent two years working on the exact 'boing' noise a device should make as you start it up.

And today, while Japanese competitors are stuttering, Samsung is notching up profits in excess of $15 billion.

Action points

- Your design process should start with the salesteam. Get them to talk to marketing and designers. Then take the challenge to the engineers or production team.

- Keep the teams apart. Many great ideas are stifled in their infancy because 'left-brain' process types are allowed to fret too early about the technical hurdles.

34

Use research like a drunk uses a lamppost*

Y ou've got a new business idea you think is a winner. The normal approach is to now put this through market research and follow the results. The world would be a much greyer one if we all followed that road.

When Dietrich Mateschitz hired a market research firm to test his new drink he was shocked at their results – they'd never had a product fail so catastrophically in testing. 'People didn't believe the taste, the logo or the brand name,' he recalls. But he launched anyway. The drink was called Red Bull and it's now the most popular energy drink in the world, selling three billion cans a year.

The problem is that your market research panel are not the best informed. Your customers often don't know they want your new product until you convince them. As Henry Ford said, 'If I had asked my customers what they wanted, they would have asked for a faster horse.'

(*i.e. more for support than illumination)

Market research is too often used as a safety net – a tool to reassure a sceptical board that a new idea is not just the lunatic hunch of a crazed inventor that's going to cost them all their jobs. Unfortunately, the best ideas often need a leap of faith.

Action points

- Don't base the success of your new idea on large-scale quantitative research exercises.
- If you need research, do it on the deep, micro level (see Rule 32: Sleep with your customers).
- If you realise you need research mainly to convince sceptical others, then think of simpler ways to do this such as buying 'off the shelf' research, or doing a competitor audit.

35
Come last

"Creativity is often just plagiarism that's gone undetected."

O pen a business magazine or management book and you won't have to flick through too many pages before the author will exhort you to grab 'first mover advantage'. It seems intuitive that in a land grab, the true prizes go to those who get there first.

But there's a reason pioneers have arrows in their backs.

The first one into a market is the one that has to make all the mistakes. They have to deal with the technology that doesn't quite work as planned, the customers who aren't quite ready for the new idea they're pitching, or converting a sceptical media.

Ideas typically take off when they reach the famous 'tipping point'; where a critical weight of opinion gathers behind a new idea and propels it into the mainstream. And often the genuine pioneer is left ruefully watching from the river bank.

A study by Peter Golder and Gerard Tellis, cited in *The Economist*, showed that over time, first-movers ended up with just seven per cent of the eventual market for their product. While the plaudits go to the pioneers, the profits are harvested by their more patient imitators.

There can be few more salutary (or amusing) examples than that of Boo.com. They launched to great hype as the future of fashion retailing on the cusp of the new millennium. However, consumers weren't quite ready to buy expensive fashion online, and their slow dial-up internet connections couldn't handle Boo's whizzy avatars. While Boo.com crashed to earth, more recent sites like Net-a-Porter.com are sweeping up the market.

'If I have seen further,' wrote Isaac Newton, 'it is only by standing on the shoulders of giants.' Well bully for you, Isaac, but I don't want to miss my chance for glory because someone else is standing on my head.

Action points

- If you've spotted a great market gap, recognise that success goes not to the one who has the idea, but the one who can successfully implement it.

- Anticipate the hurdles that exist, and look around to see who else is grappling with them.

- Follow your industry pioneers with a hawklike intensity. And when the market is ripe for the plucking, swoop in on it and dominate it with your superior version.

36
Creativity needs a sergeant major

Ready for some 'blue-sky thinking'? Are you thinking sufficiently 'outside of the box'?

Hear the term 'creatives' and an image springs to mind of floppy-haired types wafting around waiting for their muse to come to them. Companies don't help with this. In a renovation of their offices, the BBC put garden sheds in the middle of the floors so their 'creatives' could get in touch with their inner selves.

But I believe creativity benefits more from a good, sharp kick up the ass.

The brain works at it's best when caught in a tight corner. If you want to get some genuinely good ideas, then you need a sergeant major to put you under pressure to deliver them. As one silicon valley entrepreneur said recently, 'A crisis is too good an opportunity to go to waste.'

Perhaps the greatest demonstration of creative thinking under pressure began on 13 April 1970 in Houston.

An explosion in one of Apollo 13's oxygen tanks two days into their mission led to a catastrophic loss of water, power and oxygen in the spacecraft. The three-man crew were stranded 322,000 kilometres from Earth.

In Houston, NASA engineers worked out the crew's only hope of survival was in the tiny lunar landing module. However, it soon became clear that while there was sufficient oxygen in the module, it was only designed for a short two-person trip and so dangerous levels of carbon dioxide began to build up. The engineers had less than 24 hours to come up with a solution.

First, they sent the crew to dig out spare air filters in the command module, only to find these wouldn't fit the round holes of the lunar module. So using only the equipment and tools the crew had on board – including plastic Moon rock bags, cardboard, suit hoses and duct tape – they came up with a solution, and radioed instructions to the crew, along with a set of procedures to steer the module around the Moon, using its gravity as a slingshot to fire the stricken craft back to Earth.

Action points

If you face a creative challenge then try the following:

- Don't start looking for the answer. Spend time setting the parameters of the problem, including all the variables required for the ideal solution.

- Bring your team together, but put them under pressure. Set a tight deadline, don't be afraid to be critical, and chuck in additional hurdles to energise the brain to keep going.

37
Get lost

"People who have a new idea have often just ceased having an old idea."

– Edwin Land, founder of Polaroid

Sometimes the greatest block to creativity is how much you already know.

One of the most powerful drivers of human nature is habit. There is a strong evolutionary bias for this, as Charles Duhigg, author of *The Power of Habit*, observes: 'Left to its own devices, the brain will try to make almost any repeated behaviour into a habit, because habits allow our minds to conserve effort.'

Given the complexity of the modern world, our brains are hardwired to impose familiar patterns on unfamiliar solutions. It's a great approach if you're surviving in the wild. Less useful if you're trying to invent a new production process.

Modern technology isn't making this any easier. The 'Google effect' that focuses our search and reading habits means there's less room for the joyously serendipitous discovery of, say, a BBC4 documentary about electricity generation.

You need to find ways to forcibly break these habits.

One of the greatest post-war innovation hubs has been the Massachusetts Institute of Technology. An unintended ingredient of its success was a desperate shortage of space which meant disparate groups of scientists were jammed together in wooden prefab huts. The confusing layout meant they frequently got lost, and while wandering the maze of corridors would stumble upon other scientists and labs and start chatting. MIT's outputs include microwave technology, high-speed photography and the Bose speaker.

Some companies have sought to replicate this. On buying Pixar, Steve Jobs moved the company to an old factory and put the only toilets in the middle of the building, ensuring disparate employees were more likely to bump into each other.

Action points

- To stop the brain taking its habitual path, change your routine. Get off the tube a stop early. Take a different walk into work every day. Eat in a different café at lunchtime, and take your notebook.

- Leave space for serendipity in your life; 'Not all those who wander are lost,' as JRR Tolkien said.

- You can try something more radical. A researcher at Palo Alto in the 1940s tried to live to a 25-hour clock. Unfortunately, it sent him mad.

38
Fire, ready, aim

No matter how robust your research, and intuitive your reasoning, innovation requires a leap. Then you wait nervously to see what customers actually make of your idea, and whether they'll buy it.

Or you could sell your product before you've made it.

There's nothing like asking people to stump up their hard-earned cash to really test your proposition. I've learnt this from bitter experience. In my final year at university, I decided to produce a yearbook like they had in the States. When I sounded out my fellow students in the bar, they all politely enthused about my idea, and how much they'd pay.

But when the day came that I set up my stall stacked with freshly printed yearbooks, it was a different matter. All of a sudden £7 was £7 that couldn't be spent on beer and pizza, and they became a lot more discerning about what they wanted from a book before they'd pony up. (Fortunately, I found their parents were a lot less discerning on graduation day.)

So what do you do in a larger business? Surely it's impractical to put a prototype into the market?

Tech giants Intuit prove otherwise. They came up with an idea for a text-message 'marketplace' for Indian farmers to sell their products. Rather than building the system, they rigged up a simple prototype in a matter of weeks. They fulfilled the trades by hand themselves, frantically texting back and forth. They incorporated feedback and adapted until they had the ideal model. Only then did they build it.

As Intuit founder Scott Cook said, 'Sometimes you need "leadership by experiment". When the bosses make the decisions, decisions are made by politics, persuasion, and PowerPoint. When you make decisions through experiment, the best idea can prove itself.'

Action points

- Build a simple prototype of a new product or service.
- Get it into your customers' hands as soon as you can.
- Relentlessly run through iterations of change until you have perfected it.

39

Seek out your worst customers

'No, love, it doesn't make your bum look big at all.' We all know deep down that if we want a truthful answer, there's little point asking those closest to us. And yet we make that mistake all the time when it comes to market research. If you want to find out what customers genuinely think of your company, don't rely on the opinions of your biggest and best customers. Look out instead for those who are disenchanted with you. You'll have to seek them out, as they're not the ones to fill out surveys. You should also do it personally. The Chief Exec of one company I know would phone his customers as they came out of the Christmas parties. Fuelled by booze, they gave him far more honest answers than they would in the cold light of day.

Global design agency Ideo also advise companies to ignore their most typical customers. Faced with a brief for designing a new toilet brush, they ignored suburban mums and instead looked for extreme users. They found a chambermaid in Singapore who cleaned 200 toilets a day. She'd gone as far as customising her own loo brush. Ideo worked closely with her to design a new product based on her insights, and together created a loo brush that now nets over $200 million a year.

Action points

- Look through your books at the customers who've drifted away from your business, and ask them why.
- Even with your best customers, catch them off guard and dig for genuine feedback, not the usual platitudes.

40
Don't start from where you are

The lost American tourist pulls over to a Highland roadside to ask directions from a rain-drenched local. 'Say, old man, how do I get to Inverness?' 'Well, laddie,' comes the dour reply, 'I wouldn't start from here.'

The problem with going from A to C is sometimes that you get completely stuck at point B. But what if you start at C and work backwards?

The Indian government was keen to bring its rural communities online. However, the logistics of laying the cables and setting up wi-fi stations to connect them presented a massive technical challenge.

Then someone had a bright idea. The villagers were generally only interested in doing a few things online such as checking cricket scores, swapping emails with distant family members, or ordering medicines. Six times a day, a local bus passes through each village. Why not put a portable wi-fi router on the bus? As the bus drives through each village it updates pages and downloads messages to a community computer housed in a local store that locals can access.

Action points

- If you face an intractable problem, take a break from driving forwards to try to force an answer.

- Instead, start with the problem, and try redefining it in its broadest terms. What is the actual result you need to deliver, as opposed to the solution you are trying to impose? Then track backwards from this point.

41

Rip up your confidentiality agreements

You have a shiny new business or product idea. Your natural instinct is to protect your baby at all costs, hold it close to your chest and not breathe a whisper to anyone about it without them first signing an oath of secrecy with their own blood.

I wouldn't bother.

If someone's sufficiently motivated to rip you off, a piece of paper's not going to stop them. Look at Apple's experience in China, where counterfeiters had rigged up a whole network of fake Apple Stores that even the employees allegedly didn't realise were bogus. And even if you do take on the pirates, recognise the cost this will incur in terms of legal fees and the amount of your time it will take up.

Chances are, you are not the only person who has stumbled on your idea. History is littered with examples of amazing breakthroughs happening spontaneously. Charles Darwin had spent 20 years polishing the evidence to support his theory of natural selection when, in 1858, he received a request from fellow British biologist Alfred Russel

Wallace to help publish his theory on evolution, which to Darwin's great shock replicated his own.

If you are going to try to get ahead of the market, then recognise your true weapon is not secrecy, but how fast you implement your ideas, and the culture of innovation in your business. You can't risk slowing down your momentum or gumming up your culture by zealously guarding your ideas.

Action points

- If you have what you believe is a genuinely new idea, give yourself a deadline.

- Take the launch at a sprint, and get as many people behind your idea as you can to build up an unstoppable momentum.

- The returns come not to the best idea, but the person who successfully implements it.

42
Allow for the law of unintended consequences

Vain inventors may not always admit it, but some of the greatest inventions have come about by accident. A research scientist had the less-than-stellar achievement of inventing a glue that wasn't particularly glue-y. Commiserating, a colleague asked if he could use it to pin notes to his hymn book in church. And thus the Post-it note was born.

Pfizer researchers noticed that their drug Sildenafil wasn't much use at treating angina. But they noticed it had dramatic effects on other parts of their subjects' anatomy. And thus Viagra was born, and became one the most profitable prescription drugs in history.

A Finnish engineer added a 'throw-away' function to allow mobile phones to send messages by text, thinking deaf people might find it useful. This throw-away function earned telecoms companies $114.6 billion in 2011.

As they say, life is what happens when you are making other plans. You need to leave yourself time and space to get things wrong, and then be willing to act on the consequences.

And remember that the 'law of unintended consequences' can work both ways. Having installed the Shah in Iran, the US thought they'd help him by providing him with state-of-the-art intaglio printing presses for his currency. A coup later, and almost undetectable counterfeit $100 notes start to flood the US Midwest, leading the US Treasury to have to substantially redesign its currency.

Action points

- Allow space for serendipity in your life. Don't automatically discard failures but put them aside for reflection.
- If you are pushing hard towards a specific destination, keep a 'weather eye' out for the possibly unintended repercussions of your activity.

43
Remember you are French

I recently interviewed a globe-trotting French entrepreneur who'd succeeded in expanding his Paris-based events company around the world. Asking about his secrets in doing business in other countries, he answered, 'Every time I step off the plane in a foreign country I say to myself: "Pierre, remember you are French!"'

Our cultural goggles are so close to our faces, it's sometimes hard to remember we are wearing them. Our assumptions about what others find valuable or trust are so deeply ingrained, they not only lead to misunderstanding, but can blinker us to opportunity.

It can be a matter of how we do business. In the West, we might expect friendship to arise out of doing business together. In China, they expect business to potentially arise out of friendship.

More fundamentally, it can be a wholesale approach to industries. If you have a doctor in China, you pay them when you are well, but don't have to when you are sick. It may sound counter-intuitive to our way of thinking, but it makes sense. Or the Chinese vineyard owner who, when mocked about the Chinese habit of adding Coca-Cola to fine wine, retorted, 'Yes, but then you Westerners put milk in your tea.'

Action point

- Buy the Australian map that turns the globe upside down. Whenever you've going abroad, look at it to remember how much you are viewing the world through the lens of your cultural inheritance.

44
Anticipate complaints

Laura Tenison was stuck in hospital recovering from a car accident when she got chatting to the woman in the bed next to her. She was complaining about the lack of children's clothes available online. Tenison then heard other mums saying how maternity wear was dowdy and downmarket. So on leaving hospital, she set up her business JoJo Maman Bébé to provide stylish maternity wear online.

It's not news that the best business ideas can come from overhearing a customer's complaint. The only drawback is that by the time it has reached the stage people are openly grumbling about a problem, chances are others will have already spotted it and you'll be lucky to get just a couple of steps ahead.

According to Apple's head design honcho Jonathan Ive, the secret is to *anticipate* complaints. You have to look at a product or service and imagine what, in the future, an ideal user would find frustrating with it, even if they don't know it now. This echoes the advice of Canadian ice hockey champion Wayne Gretzky: 'Skate to where the puck's going, not where it is.'

It means not looking at the current state of things, but looking forwards months and even years to imagine a future world, and customers' hopes and frustration. Doing it means you can invent a whole new category of products that redefines your industry.

Action points

- Put on your negative head. Gather a group of co-workers and really pull your industry and business apart.
- Then see if you can get ahead of the competition by rebuilding it in your image.

45
Get stotious

Blitzed, blootered, bombed – there are few parts of the English language that are as rich as terms for getting drunk. I also believe that getting banjoed can be a path to profit.

To be more precise, not the actual drunk bit. Obviously lunatic ideas can suddenly take on a veneer of credibility when fuelled by four pints of Stella (like my colleague's surprising brainwave one evening that we should all snog each other 'so we wouldn't waste energy at work being curious').

It's the morning after when the best ideas can strike. I have no scientific evidence to back this up other than my own personal experience. However, on 'normal' days I seem to have an internal policeman in my head who sense-checks my more outlandish thoughts and vetoes them before I can give them oxygen. I think we all have this – it's what Freud would call our 'Super Ego'. I see mine as a strict German schoolmistress, but that's another story.

But somehow, the effects of a mild hangover seem to knock her out. All of a sudden I have these flights of creative fancy. I keep a notebook to hand and I let my mind wander. I sketch out the hurdles we face at work, and let my imagination run free without fear of reprimand. It's the best internal brainstorm you can have.

And if you don't drink, try to find an activity that gives you the same state of mind where your critical faculties are turned off. I often find it out running, or in those evanescent moments between sleep and waking.

Action points

- Six pints, notebook, Alka-Seltzer.
- Job done.

46
Ban the brainstorm

E ven if we're supposed to call it a 'thought shower'
nowadays, the brainstorm has been the default
innovation engine in companies since its unwitting
invention by advertising man Alex Osborn in the 1950s.

However, as creativity maven Jonah Lehrer has pointed
out, empirical research consistently shows it doesn't work.
As early as 1958, an experiment at Yale University revealed
that groups who first worked on their own before coming
together to pool ideas produced twice as many ideas as
groups that brainstormed.

There's also a problem with the central tenet of the brainstorm, 'don't criticise other people's ideas'. It certainly makes
for very polite meetings. Unfortunately, criticism works.

If you sit back in a meeting nodding politely at every half-
baked idea, you're not fully engaged. But if while advancing
your idea, a colleague chips in with an additional hurdle to
your suggestion, your brain has to peddle a little bit harder.
And the quality of the ideas start to improve.

Action points

**If you want to wring the most from the collected
brain power at your disposal – and you'd be a fool not to –
I humbly offer you a 'Devil's Advocate' approach:**

- Individually brief each member of your team. Set the objective, but also spell out what you see as the four main challenges they have to overcome (though they're allowed to disagree with these).

- Get them to work on the problem individually for 40 minutes (that's the most a brain can concentrate optimally).

- Come together for a session to pool your ideas. Again, give it a deadline – no more than 30 minutes.

- Appoint a 'Devil's Advocate'. Their job is to facilitate the session by stopping loud-mouths trampling on quieter bits of inspiration, and keeping the discussion moving.

- Start presenting your ideas. You are absolutely allowed to disagree with each other, but you must do it in a way that a) details your reason for dissent and b) advances the challenge (e.g. not 'That would never work and you're an idiot' but 'I don't think that would work because our customers won't pay that much, but could we do it cheaper?').

- Don't try to reach a consensus decision – they always involve compromise. One person is in charge of picking the solution. It's their judgement call to take the best of what's on the table and use it if they feel like it.

47
Steal with pride

Possibly the greatest taboo in business is copying. So I'm going to steal this idea from British business luminary, Sir Eric Peacock.

Like a number of leading entrepreneurs, Sir Eric spends a few weeks every year seeking out interesting companies. 'I blag my way in and spend time with the leadership team,' says Sir Eric. 'Then I can steal with pride, and adapt with glee for my own environment and pragmatically implement fresh ideas.'

As well as picking up leadership secrets, this copying mantra can apply to whole business models. You see it in TV with 'lookee-likee' shows such as *The X Factor* and *Pop Idol*, or in the restaurant business, where new entrants are advised to open shop next to an already successful outlet.

Perhaps the most ruthless, and vilified, exponents of this approach are Germany's Samwer brothers. They have built a track record of relentlessly cloning internet business ideas from America, and replicating them fast in other non-English speaking countries.

Starting in Silicon Valley, they originally thought eBay would work in Germany and so emailed the company. When they didn't get a reply, they returned to Germany and started from scratch. Within 100 days of going live, they sold their site to eBay for £35 million. As they explain of their model, 'Someone else is the architect, we are the builders.'

It may seem shameful and somehow self-defeating to imitate, but very few ideas in business are genuinely original. It would be naïve to overlook the fact that success comes from those who can steal with pride, and implement with brilliance.

Action points

- Take time out to go and meet with the genuine innovators in your industry.

- Do it with pride – tell them in advance what you'd like to do, and treat it as a genuine opportunity to share ideas and thinking.

Part four
Sales and marketing

48
Stop making sense

Consumers are bombarded with marketing. When pitching for attention, you need to make your offer crystal clear, so the customer instantly gets the point.

But what if it's that very roar of competing noise that renders an obvious advert almost worthless?

Psychologists in the 1940s highlighted the 'Gestalt effect'. On receiving incomplete information, the brain works hard to impose a logical shape to it. Once it's made it fit into a familiar pattern, it shelves the information away.

The problem with your 'obvious advert' is that the brain understands it instantly. And it just as instantly ignores it.

But when it meets a message that doesn't fit an existing mental template, it goes into overdrive. It worries at the piece of information like a frantic dog trying to run through a half-metre gap carrying a one-metre stick.

That's exactly the effect you want your ads to have. And 'sensible' just ain't going to get you there.

The 'father of modern advertising', David Ogilvie once faced a problem trying to sell Hathaway shirts. He had a handsome model and polished copy, but the response was mediocre at best. So he gave the model an eye-patch. Customers were hooked by the intrigue. How had he lost his eye? Was it in a daring duel or a bad moment with an office stapler? Sales of Hathaway shirts shot up, and an advertising legend was born.

Ogilvy's belief was that your advertising message should act like a burr that sticks to your subconscious. You only have to look at today's drumming gorillas and rakish meerkats to see that wisdom still holds true.

Action points

- Look for a 'burr' in your branding. Something that doesn't make obvious sense, and makes your audience work harder.

- Execute your advertising professionally. If it looks homemade and slapdash, your customers won't make the effort.

49
Don't give your customers choice

W e're told today's consumer is a choice-hungry free agent, always looking to switch to a better deal. If you don't keep pace with them and offer them loads of choice and extras, they'll ditch you.

But this overlooks a deeper truth. Customers want choice, but they don't want to *have* to choose.

Making decisions is hard. Every time you have to make a choice between two alternatives, there's a risk that you'll pick the wrong one. And that's stressful.

In behavioural finance, this is known as 'regret theory'. As Professor Meir Statman observed with investment planning, if a client is faced with too many funds to choose from, they fear making the wrong choice and end up picking none. The same effect is seen when investors hold on to losing shares for too long, or slavishly follow investment fads.

But the effect is just as powerful in other sectors. Psychologists at Columbia University set up a display of jams in a Californian grocery store. In the first test they offered shoppers the choice of six different jams, the next day shoppers were given 24 to choose from. They discovered that although more people stopped at the larger display, only 3 per cent purchased. However, when only six jams were on display, 30 per cent purchased.

So you must give customers the *illusion* of choice. Leave them feeling that they're in no way pressured to purchase the offer you are targeting them with. But in reality, you want to effectively signpost their decisions towards a narrow range of products you actually want them to buy. Then after they've made their purchase, you must make a big effort to reassure them that they've made the right choice.

Action points

- Get up to speed with the startling findings of behavioural economics – a great starting point is *Thinking, Fast and Slow* by Daniel Kahneman.

- Make sure your business strikes the right balance between a framework of choice and guiding your customers to a place of reassurance.

50

Learn from the Wizard of Oz

You need to play straight with your customers if you're to build a lasting relationship. But that doesn't mean you can't sometimes use of a little bit of smoke and mirrors.

The reason for this is that customers often don't want the best. They want the least worst. They're fearful about taking a risky decision, even if they know it's a good offer. And as IBM played up in their old adverts, 'No one ever got fired for buying IBM'. IBM's labs even researched exhaustively into the exact shade of blue for their logo that would most reassure customers.

So while not being dishonest, we all have to strive to be someone before we actually become them.

In the early days of my marketing agency, we were pitching for a big account. The client liked our ideas, and we knew we could deliver. But we were small, and the client wanted to come and check us out.

So the four of us cast around for friends and family. A week later, the client came into a bustling, prosperous office full of people typing orders and buying and selling things on the phone. They didn't seem to question how we appeared to have employed a set of twins, or that a couple of 'employ-ees' were having great difficulty operating a mouse.

But we won the work, we delivered, and we haven't looked back.

Action points

- Safety matters. Do everything you can to reassure your potential customers.

- Ensure consistency in your brand, including smaller items like company outfits, stationery or talking about 'we' more than 'me' if your are self-employed.

- You could go as far as the storage entrepreneur who took the 'smoke and mirrors' approach literally. Worried that his depot wouldn't look busy enough, he put mirrors at the end of every stack so it looked twice as big to prospective clients.

51
Don't 'do' social media

Social media is the new new thing. This month, Pinterest is what we all must all 'get' for fear of being left behind. No doubt by the time this book is out, it will have been supplanted by something even shinier.

You can probably guess my take on this. I heard it described beautifully by the guys at *Contagious* magazine as the "'Dude, we've got to get a...' Syndrome', echoing the cry of panicking marketers not wanting to be left out.

You shouldn't 'do' anything, and certainly not social media.

There is only one way to approach social media, or indeed any new way of doing things. You should only do it if it's a more efficient way of delivering something you already do.

Kogi BBQ in Los Angeles is a mobile food-van business. Like most mobile vendors, they need to alert customers to where they are. So as the trucks drive around the city, the company uses Twitter to update customers on the van's location, what the specials are and what the queues are like so they don't have to hang around. They have 54,000 followers on Twitter tracking their lunch.

On the flip side, I've seen companies set up a social network in the hope that all their customers and staff will suddenly want to start sharing their thoughts online, when they've shown not the slightest inclination to do so in the past.

Action points

- When faced with a new technology, ask yourself the question, 'How can this more efficiently replace something we already do?'
- If you can't see how it can, then smile and nod politely to the enthusiasts but back away.

52
Recommend your competitors

The proud head of marketing of a global company showed me a floor full of her staff. 'Who's responsible for customer loyalty?' I asked. She paused; 'I think we have half a person.'

Assuming she wasn't talking literally, that's not unusual. Companies spend a huge amount of effort attracting new customers, while completely overlooking the value of their existing loyal customers. Typically an existing customer is easier to service, will pay higher prices, and is five times easier to sell to.

And in building this bond of loyalty, the most important currency you have is trust.

While most customers will expect you to target new offers at them, they need to know they're not being sold to at all costs. Inevitably, there will be times when your offer is not the best one for them. Then you have to do the right thing and tell them where to go, even if it means recommending a competitor.

It will mean forgoing some short-term profits, and a risk they'll form a relationship with a new supplier. But the bond of trust you will forge with them in doing this will more than compensate. And they may still decide to forgo the better offer and stick with you regardless.

By the same token, don't knock your competition. Doing so smacks of desperation, and makes you look like a backstabber. There's also the chance that your prospect has purchased from them, so you risk making them look bad. (That said, if *they* start to slag them off, it's fine to maintain an inscrutable smile.)

Action points

- Calculate the possible lifetime value of your best customers if they keep purchasing from you. That'll put things in perspective.

- Let your team know that what matters is the long-term loyalty of customers, even if that means forgoing short-term sales.

- If you are weak in a particular area, don't fudge it, but try to form a strategic alliance with a company who can provide this, without cannibalising your business.

53

If you're pitching to win – you've already lost

There are few more pivotal moments in business than the pitch. In the space of an hour millions of pounds, and the working lives of thousands can be decided.

So faced with a big pitch, you'll work hard on your credentials, on coaching your team and rehearsing so that in your alloted 60 minutes you'll dazzle the prospective client.

But I'm here to tell you that if you are walking into that room resting on your pitching ability in order to win, you've already lost. The truth is that most large pitches are won or lost long before the presentation.

Neil Flett, the CEO of global pitch consultants Rogen, describes a client who'd received a pitch invitation from a major prospect. They worked through three sets of written proposals, two major presentations and a host of interviews until the big shoot-out.

Despite a great presentation and credentials, they were blown out of the water. On debriefing, they discovered the winner had set up a project team and had been working with the client on related projects two years *before* the invitation went out. 'Our client may have played a strong second half,' says Flett, 'but the winner had been 25 points ahead before we walked out onto the field!'

Action points

- If you have no relationship, no chance to build one or no unique insight into what the client might want, then think twice before accepting a pitch invitation.

- If you get a chance to ask questions beforehand, don't use it to gather information – get that from other sources. Instead, use the opportunity to demonstrate to your prospect how much you understand their business.

- Don't keep your powder dry and save all your ideas for the big day. Sound them out with the prospect in advance so they have already bought in.

54
Be brief, be brilliant, be gone

"No one cares how much you know, until they know how much you care."

– Ralph Waldo Emerson

Faced with an invitation to pitch, the temptation is to throw everything at it. You'll want to involve as many team members as possible, and ensure you cover every base and possible permutation. Then you'll spend days or weeks crunching this down into a slick and compressed presentation.

But stop for a moment to think of the poor people on the other side of the table.

Our ability to digest information is not as great as we might imagine. A reasonable statistical baseline is research by German psychologist Hermann Ebbinghaus which shows that we forget 60 per cent of learned information just an hour after the learning takes place.

It's not just a matter of reducing the amount of text in your PowerPoint, or jazzing it up with graphics. Stop and think; what is the single thing you want to be remembered for after your presentation? Start with that, and strip out the rest. The most important decision in your pitch is what you don't say.

Perhaps the world's highest value pitch is to host the Olympics. Faced with the opportunity, one bidding nation started by thinking about the people on the awarding committee. Surely their greatest worry is that the Olympics money will be squandered on vast white elephant stadiums and crumbling edifices that leave a terrible memory of the Olympics. So the team built their pitch around the legacy it would leave with the country's children.

In the run-up to the pitch, they got a series of local primary schools to 'adopt' a member of the voting committee. Every week, the children would write a letter explaining what the bid meant to them. The night before their pitch, they left a teddy bear in each member's room with a handwritten note from the children. When they started their pitch, they didn't kick off with a slick movie or a presidential address. They started with the children walking in, and telling in their own simple words what the Olympics would mean to their lives. They won.

Action points

- Start your pitch planning not with an analysis about what's brilliant in your business, but an assessment of what your audience wants to hear.

- Focus your presentation around no more than three simple points. Test it with strangers, and ask them an hour later how the presentation made them feel.

- If you need technical proof and information, fine, but leave it in the appendix.

55
Don't hire a
hotshot agency

Your competitors are outgunning you. They're making you look dull and pedestrian. What you really need is a breakthrough advertising campaign. You need to hire the hottest agency to do it for you, and put your upstart competitors back in their place.

In truth, while there are many amazing and creative people in agencies, there's one thing that stands in front of a great creative campaign – a great client.

Ask most agencies to show you the best campaigns they've devised, and I bet they'll open a bottom drawer to show you the stuff that never got commissioned.

Long before you start hunting out and briefing hotshot creatives, you need to get your own house in order. You need to have a very clear brief. Can you really aspire to being a challenger brand, or will that risk you looking like your dad dancing? Do you have the authority to commission this campaign, and if not, have you sounded out those who have so you won't get 'death by committee'?

Just look at Microsoft. Riled by Apple's successful 'Mac vs PC' advertising campaign, they turned to hotshot agency Crispin, Porter + Bogusky to produce its $300 million 'I'm a

PC' television ad campaign. It showed everyday people to be
PC users, but served mainly to enhance Apple's brand awareness and emphasise the difference between the two firms.

Action points

- If you want to change your brand's personality, then
  don't start by painting the outside walls. First, honestly
  appraise who you are, and what a realistic aspiration for
  your company is. If you want to stretch this, then work
  on your culture first.

- Only then should you set about hiring an agency. And
  look for one that's a realistic reflection of who you
  are, not a shot-in-the dark aspiration for who your
  competitors are.

56

Put the small print in BIG LETTERS

L ife is full of risk. I believe we should be more honest with our customers about risks, and what might go wrong if they buy from us.

Don't worry, I'm not coming over all touchy-feely and ethical. God forbid. My rationale is far more prosaic. You should do it simply because it will win you more business.

The problem is that we don't apply the same standards to our customers as we do to ourselves.

As purchasers, when we're faced with an unbelievable offer, an alarm bell starts ringing in our head that there HAS to be a catch. And yet when it comes to selling our products, our natural inclination is to sugar-coat things, and pretend it's all risk-free. And guess what? The customer doesn't believe us!

So why not do things the other way around? After you've explained your offer, spend time telling your customer all the things that could go wrong. As Ted Wang, a lawyer from California, says in *Inc.* magazine: 'Sometimes, when I circulate an investor questionnaire, I put in bold, all caps, **YOU COULD LOSE ALL YOUR MONEY**. If people are not comfortable with that, they shouldn't invest.'

And then a strange thing happens. Our brains are wired to find solutions to problems. If you are telling someone everything is going to be all rosy, their unconscious starts motoring through all the ways it might not be.

But if you present the problems up front, the process flips and their mind starts working out ways round these problems. They sell themselves on your idea.

Action points

- Try being more modest in your promotions and credential presentations.

- Put your small print in big letters at the start. Be direct and honest. Customers will then file that away and concentrate on what you are selling, without automatically discounting everything you say.

57
Dull is the new sexy

D on't let the creatives run your sales pitches.

Ask a creative person, and they'll always want to do something new and creative. It's what drives them, and what wins awards. Most of the time, that hunger is fantastic. But sometimes it's the last thing you need.

You need to really understand your customers, and what it is they're buying from you. Is it glory? Is it getting chatted up at the awards ceremony? Or do they just want to keep paying the mortgage every month?

I've listened to countless businesspeople recount how they've been asked by prospects for 'something innovative'. When they offer that, they get rejected because 'it's never been done before'. As one businessman eloquently put it to me, 'If I hear someone ask for something innovative again, I'll punch them in the face.'

It is a little known law in publishing that every business book must have a Branson anecdote. Here's mine: the great bearded one was pitching to run the National Lottery. Naturally, his approach was for a new and exciting 'People's Lottery', and he set about drumming up the hype. But he overlooked that he was pitching to civil servants. There was no 'upside' for these people for all the hoopla Branson was generating. But there was a very considerable downside if he cocked up. So they plumped instead for his dull but safe competitors.

Action points

- Try to establish what your prospect's actual hopes and fears are, and pitch accordingly.
- It doesn't mean you have to be boring. A bit of pizazz and fairy dust in the delivery can make even the dullest offer sparkle.

58
Make your
literature illegible

You've come up with a compelling offer for your customers. Surely you want to communicate it so clearly that your customers will understand it with the minimum of effort?

Surprisingly, it works the other way. In the same way that obvious adverts sail right past us (see Rule 48: Stop making sense), literature that's too easy to read does just the same.

To test the hypothesis, researchers at Princeton University asked two groups of volunteers to read the same piece of text. One version was clear and easy to read, but with the second group, they deliberately shrunk the text size and put it in an annoyingly hard-to-read Comic Sans font. When tested later, the group with the hard text remembered 14 per cent more of it.

The more of an effort someone has to make to digest information, the more that message becomes embedded in their memory.

And 'signalling theory' is also at work. In the same way that women appreciate men buying them flowers and not electrical gadgets because they recognise the extra effort the man has had to make, if you dumb down your literature to the extent that even a seven-year-old on a sugar rush can read it, you are signalling to your customers that it's not worth the effort.

Action points

- Take your customers seriously. If what you have to say is important, then don't dumb it down. Ask them to make the extra effort.
- That's no excuse for lazy writing or poor design. As Einstein said, 'Make it as simple as possible, but no simpler.'

59
Nurture your nutters

As we become numb to marketing messages, there's one source that's still trusted above all others – a personal recommendation from someone we trust. Despite what marketing wizards might promise, this is not something you can buy. Sure, social media can streamline the recommendation process, but just getting customers to click a 'Like' button isn't the answer. Research on the World Advertising Research Centre website showed that just 0.5 per cent of customers actively engage with brands they 'like' on Facebook.

Rather than being 'liked', why not turn your business into one that customers rave about?

It helps if you start with a personal level of passion that borders on the obsessional. Take Morgan sports cars. A motorist wanting to buy one of the hand-tailored wooden-framed cars has to put down a hefty deposit and then wait up to a year for delivery. But there is no shortage of enthusiasts happy to wait and to pay a premium for British craftsmanship.

You don't have to be selling luxury goods. Murray Lender is credited with making America fall in love with the bagel. His passion took the humble bun from his father's bakery store to a national staple. Even being rendered mute by a stroke 13 years ago did not stop his evangelical mission, such as composing songs for the sales reps to sing.

You can also build passion into your delivery. Creating raving fans is not about delivering '100 per cent satisfaction' but by creating 'wow' moments of delight that stand out. The simplest way to start this is by under-promising, and over-delivering. Getting your order to the customer a couple of days before you said you would, and bundling in extras, is exactly the kind of thing to get you talked about.

Action points

- Don't apologise for being a nerd about your product. Your enthusiasm is infectious (even if people start to back away from your mad, staring eyes at parties).

- Look for customer 'moments of truth' when they really experience your product or service (e.g. when they first check in at your hotel). Think what you can do to turn these into 'wow' points that customers rave about.

- Tell your story. People buy people, so let them into your world.

START WITH A PERSONAL

...THAT BORDERS ON THE

LEVEL OF PASSION...

OBSESSIONAL.

60

Create a crisis

The traditional sales process is about putting your customer's mind at ease. You take time to understand them, build a relationship of trust, and reassure them they're making the right choice.

Or you could opt to scare the crap out of them.

Just as having too much time to complete a project means you delay finishing it (as I found when I got a month's extension on this text), sometimes there are powerful reasons to push customers into thinking fast and intuitively about a purchase.

Perhaps the greatest exponent of this art is Beanie Babies.

Ignoring early critics who called his soft toys 'road kill', Ty Warner understood almost better than anyone the power of scarcity.

He started to nurture 'sought after' status for his Beanie Babies soft toys by only selling to niche stores, and deliberately limiting the number each store was allowed to buy – 36 of each character per month. If a store sold out, tough luck. Fans would have to wait another month.

Ty then started to ramp up the pressure by 'retiring' certain characters. Beanie prices shot up wildly as collectors realised the value of scarcity. Some characters changed hands for as much as $6,000 (for soft toys which had originally retailed at $5). Sales continued to soar as fans, knowing that some characters could disappear at any time, tried to snap up as many Beanies as possible.

Ty had one more trick up his sleeve – in August 1999, he announced that the company would stop making Beanie Babies at 11.59 pm on 31 December of that year. It sent buyers into a frenzy of panic purchasing. In the end Ty relented, saying customers could save the Beanies from extinction if fans voted on the internet to save them, which, of course, they dutifully flocked to do in their droves.

It might seem harsh, but bear in mind that in 1999 Ty Inc. surpassed Mattel and Hasbro to become the largest toy company in the US.

Action points

- While there is no honour in resorting to 'boiler room' sales tactics, bear in mind that scarcity sends out a primeval hording signal to consumers.

- Perhaps highlight any genuine scarcity behind producing your product or service. Or put the skates on your customers by highlighting what their competition is up to.

61
Shut up

"We're adding a little something to this month's sales contest. As you all know, first prize is a Cadillac Eldorado. Anybody want to see second prize? Second prize is a set of steak knives. Third prize is you're fired."

– Blake, *Glengarry Glen Ross*

I f you want a course in traditional sales techniques, then watch Alec Baldwin terrorise a sales force in the film *Glengarry Glen Ross*.

You need a slick patter. You'll have honed it to the point you can do it in your sleep. For every objection, you have a well-weighted choice of responses. Every step the customer takes, you're hustling them towards The Close.

And that's why your customers have a waxy glaze on their faces as you spout. It's why they hang up on your calls. It's why they don't dare set foot in your store in the first place.

Your smart answers and clever sales techniques aren't working. You need to shut up and listen to your customers; they have some interesting things to say. What's more, they are fed up with you trying to talk them into a sale. In fact, the more you try, the more they'll dig their heels in.

Twenty-first century salespeople let the customers sell themselves.

From Wikipedia to TripAdvisor, we're riding on the crest of what author Clay Shirky dubbed 'cognitive surplus'. Consumers are no longer passive drones to be shunted towards your choice. They want a share in creating the solution themselves.

To win them over, show them your half-finished ideas, your 'starting-off' points not your polished answers. Then engage them in co-creating and customising their own desired solutions.

It was a technique I learnt from an English teacher. In a moment of poor deadline planning, I padded an essay by lifting a verbatim chunk of what he'd said in class that day. Imagine my surprise when it came back with an 'A' grade, with his comment, 'Such penetrating insight!'

Action points

- Design a sales framework that allows your customers space to tailor their own solutions.
- You have two ears and one mouth – use them in that proportion.

62
Get your face slapped

You remember that boy at school? Never the most blessed in the looks department or in their genetic inheritance, but they always seemed to end up with the best-looking girl.

However many hours you spend fine-tuning your sales and marketing pitch, take a lesson from that boy at school; you'll get more snogs by being Mr Right Now than in trying to be Mr Right.

The most important factor in sales is timing. That means it's a numbers game, and while you'll get your face slapped occasionally, the ones who win are those who keep knocking at the door, and learn not to take rejection personally. Ask Walt Disney.

Putting down the novel *Mary Poppins*, Walt knew it would make a fantastic film. He got in touch with the author Pamela Travers but she knocked him back. A film wouldn't do justice to her creation she believed, and certainly not one made by a man who, at the time, had only a string of cartoons behind him.

Walt wasn't a person to be easily put off. Over the next 16 years, he travelled repeatedly to her home in England to persuade her. Eventually won over by his protestations, she relented. The resulting film won five Academy Awards, was nominated for eight others and remains a classic to this day.

Action points

- Work out your hit ratio from your sales calls. If you are not failing at least 50 per cent of the time, then you are not trying hard enough.
- If the continual rejections are starting to depress you, work out what it is about them that upsets you. Then examine why the customer is saying 'no'. It's not that they don't like your winning ways, it's probably because they don't perceive a need, are concerned about cost, or the timing is wrong. Work on fixing those reasons.

63

It's only worth advertising on your forehead

W e live in a world of noise:

- Every year, companies in the UK spend over £40 billion on direct marketing.
- 70 per cent of the world's email traffic is spam.
- Consumers see 3,000 marketing messages a day.
- Google currently searches over eight billion web pages.

It's a thankless task to try and buy recognition for your brand. It'll take many years and many millions to hammer your message into your customers' subconscious. And the more we take the sledgehammer approach, the more resistant customers become.

If you're a global multinational, then that route might be fine. The rest of us need to think creatively.

To get through the cacophony of competing noise, you need to stand out. And one way to do that is to turn the medium into the message.

Daunted by their £50,000 student debts, Cambridge graduates Ed Moyse and Ross Harper hit on the wheeze of selling advertising space on their own faces. Through their business, 'Buy My Face', anyone can pay a few hundred pounds to have their business advertised on the friends' faces for a day. People can also see the ads by logging onto their website. So far the pair have made over £30,000.

Accountancy giant PwC were looking to boost their credentials in the not-for-profit sector. Rather than buying ad space, they bought the old fire station next to their office. They then rented this out to social enterprises as an incubator for their businesses.

Action points

- What is the *essence* of your company's brand? Thinking visually, what ways could you bring these values to life in the real world rather than just on paper?
- Take inspiration from the thinking of others; there are some great books and websites on 'Guerrilla Marketing'.

64
Fake sincerity

'Have a nice day,' intones the slack-jawed teenager as they slide over your Mega Burger. 'Iseverythingalrightwithyourmeal?' mumbles the stressed waitress as you chew your first mouthful.

Of all the creeping Americanisations of our culture, the enforced chumminess of 'customer-service' staff is surely the most reviled. We Brits don't want waiters to be our friends. We just want no-nonsense impersonal service.

Only it appears we don't.

I travel a lot for work, and whenever I go into a Prêt A Manger, I'm touched by the casual and solicitous way the staff engage me in a bit of banter or ask how my day is. And as they say, once you can fake sincerity, you've got it made.

But it doesn't happen by accident. Pret spend almost £10 million every year sending a team of mystery shoppers into every branch, every week, to monitor customer service. Staff are encouraged to offer you a glass of water on a hot day, or compliment you on your earrings. And to ensure the behaviours are sincere, the team is rewarded accordingly. Cash bonuses are awarded for teams, not individuals. When an employee reaches a target, they must pass on the reward vouchers to their most supportive colleague. New recruits are also vetted by their fellow store members and given a thumbs up or down if they should stay.

In a lovely twist, they are now exporting this model to their stores in the States.

And as to the 'Is-everything-fine-with-your-meal?' brigade, I'm told this is only to stop you waiting 'til the end of the meal to complain so you can ask for your money back.

Action points

- Ensure your team have 'skin in the game'; they share in the success and rewards from the whole team's performance. Then give them the chance to appraise their peers and vote on new recruits.

- Consider mystery shoppers, and grade colleagues on how pleasant they are when they interact with your customers.

Part five
Staff

65

Pay your staff to quit

As a harassed boss, you bend over backwards to keep your team happy and stop them jumping ship.

But staff retention, particularly amongst Generation X workers, isn't what it was. 'If you want loyalty,' say the experts, 'get a Labrador.'

And given it can cost upto £5,000 to find, recruit and fully train a new employee, those wandering feet can hit you with a big bill.

You need to know from the get-go that your new recruits are committed. So why not put it to the test?

In building Zappos into a billion-dollar online shoe retailer, Tony Hsieh knew stunning customer service would be the 'magic sauce' of his success. So during their lengthy training and induction programme, Tony offers any employee $2,000 to quit. As he says, 'It's essential to know early on if an employee doesn't buy into our vision. Testing that commitment just makes economic sense.'

It's testament to his judgement that 97 per cent turn down that offer.

Action points

- Make sure you spend time with new recruits, selling them on the vision and 'secret sauce' of the business.
- Offer them a financial incentive to quit during this period. This level of commitment from you will be matched by the commitment they'll repay you with.

66
Money doesn't motivate

In the last decade we've witnessed the greatest increase in income inequality in history. It now seems accepted wisdom that in order to keep your 'talent' loyal, you have to offer them increasingly eye-watering sums to stop the footloose from jumping ship.

Yet the more prosaic truth is that money is a poor motivator.

In his fantastic book, *Drive: The Surprising Truth About What Motivates Us,* Daniel Pink cites research by economists at MIT, funded by the Federal Reserve Bank, which demonstrated that for 'brain workers' (as opposed to purely manual workers), a larger financial reward led to a poorer performance.

There is a minimum you have to pay; an amount that, as Pink says, 'takes money off the table'. But beyond that, not only does extra pay not drive better performance, it can drive behaviours in the wrong direction.

What knowledge workers value more highly are three things: autonomy, mastery of their task and a sense of deeper purpose to what they do.

Action points

- Make sure your company's pay is fair. You might not be able to match the very top payers in your industry, but pay enough that colleagues feel they're not being taken advantage of.

- Ditch pay as your only way of rewarding outstanding performance.

- Instead, consider introducing things like 'Free Play Time', when staff get to work on whatever creative project they like, regardless of its possible immediate use in the business.

- Then get the hell out of their way.

67

Hire some baboons

In the animal kingdom, baboons are masters of all they survey. Obsessed by status, they swagger around the place with puffed chests and an inordinate pride in their big red bottoms.

Pretty much like salespeople then.

Salespeople have a tendency to wind up the rest of a company. They don't play by the rules, they can be arrogant, inconsiderate, boastful, greedy and lazy. Yet without them, your business is dead in the water. I say this with the greatest respect as a salesperson myself.

I heard of a leading magazine publisher going through hoops to keep their top salesman sweet. Flouting all company policies, he had previously managed to wangle himself a Porsche as his company car. But now he decided he wanted a Lamborghini.

After much apoplexy from the finance director, they bought him one. As they all stood around admiring it, the MD put his hand out for the Porsche keys. The salesman looked him straight in the eye and said, 'Who said anything about *swap*?'

The situation was clearly untenable, and the company let the salesman go. He then went off to start, build and sell a £60 million publishing company and is currently spending his retirement in the Bahamas.

Action points

- You need to hire yourself the baddest baboons in the whole jungle. Ideally you need two or more as they're naturally competitive.

- Be prepared to rip up your employment handbook, so long as they keep delivering.

- Keep them well apart from the rest of the employees.

68
Don't recruit by experience

You're making a vital new hire for your business. Sitting opposite you is someone who has done the same job for a competitor. They can slot straight in. Sure, they might not set the heather alight, but they're the safe bet.

Hang fire.

It's understandable to want to hire a safe pair of hands. Chances are you don't have time to train someone up, or wait for them to get up to speed. But bear in mind this: you can train most skills in a business. What you can't train is attitude. And it's that attitude that will make or break your business.

In 1972 a Liverpool schoolboy was keen to earn some cash but there were no jobs around. So he travelled to London and got a job at the Wandsworth branch of Tesco. He started by filling the tea and coffee machine, and progressed to shelf-stacker and floor-washer. 'It seemed a busy, friendly place but a bit rough around the edges,' he remembers.

By the time he retired from Tesco in 2011, the same schoolboy, now knighted as Sir Terry Leahy, had led Tesco from a market follower to one of the world's largest retailers with profits of £2 billion.

In taking a 'retread' from your competition, there's a risk your new recruit will have a load of bad habits you'll have to get them to unlearn. They might also not feel stretched by your role, which is vital.

It's a great motivator for other employees to be in a business that 'grows its own timber', where someone can rise from the very bottom to the top by merit of their own effort and ability, and where management are not blinded by 'rock star résumés' of potential new recruits.

Action points

- When hiring, make sure you have a big tick on your scorecard for attitude.

- With an experienced recruit, question the extent to which they might be bored with the role you're offering.

- Could a hungry young schoolkid rise to lead your company? If not, what's blocking them?

- Work out career progression plans for all your key team members. Give them exposure to big risk and responsibility situations wherever you can.

69
Forget the big idea

Too many businesspeople are looking for the cure for cancer. They want the one ground-breaking idea that will transform the industry. It's all very well for the ego, but it's not very good for the bank balance.

The more useful type of innovation is far more granular. These are the small, unapplauded ideas around process or packaging that can end up saving your company thousands. And most often they're to be found on the shop floor, not in the C-suite.

Look at the factory worker who saved Swan Vesta thousands of pounds by pointing out to his employers that they only needed to put sandpaper on one side of their matchboxes. Money-saving ideas are potentially floating around your business; you just need a more efficient way to capture them than the dusty Suggestion Box sitting in the works canteen.

In 2008, the Minnesota-based Mayo Clinic found that costs were running ahead of income. So it turned to staff to help turn things around through an employee-run ideas website. One department showed how switching off non-essential electrical devices would save them $900,000, and another moved employee directories online, saving a further $100,000.

Action points

- Set your teams the challenge of finding a targeted amount of savings in a year.

- Look at the process for capturing, evaluating and recognising these achievements.

- While cash never offends, think of other rewards for the best ideas.

70
Drive a clunker

Y ou've done well. You've risen to the top by your own efforts. It's time you rewarded yourself with a big, shiny, new car.

I guarantee it'll end up being the most expensive car you'll ever buy.

The reason you've been successful is because you've taken other people with you. They've made huge efforts on your behalf to build the business.

So, you're all in it together, working towards a common goal, and then you suddenly pitch up driving a Porsche. What do you think that's going to do to everyone's motivation?

I'm not saying you shouldn't enjoy the fruits of your labours and a reward for all the risks you've taken. All I'm saying is the price you will have to add to everyone's salary, or the subsequent drop in performance, could end up costing you thousands of pounds.

I was slack-jawed in amazement to read recently about an entrepreneur whose staff perk was for the week's top performer to be allowed to drive his flash car around the car park.

And what about your clients? An old competitor of ours drove into an NHS client's car park in his lovely top-of-the-range Jaguar. But as they watched in envy from the windows, he proceeded to get it wedged tight on a low brick wall he'd not spotted.

Far better to copy the mission statement of a young design agency: 'Macs not Mercs.'

Action points

- If you want a treat, then practise 'inconspicuous consumption'. Far better to have your money going into a sailing boat sitting discreetly in a harbour than on a flash sports car that gets spat at when you're stuck in a traffic jam.

- Or practise some self-restraint; achievement is its own reward. Invest your profits back into the business so you build an enterprise that's there for the long term.

71

Take your name off the door

"Name on the door, trouble in't store."

– Yorkshire expression

Watch any US TV show and you'll know someone's made it when they reach the corner office. They can measure their worth by carpet acreage and how far they can putt their executive golf balls on this hallowed turf.

But the moment you make that move into your sound proofed citadel is the moment problems will start.

A journalist was comparing the success of UK supermarkets. As he visited each he was faced with the standard protocol used by big companies of having to navigate his way through an intimidating corporate fortress, clambering around various minions before encountering the liege lord or lady.

His final stop was Tesco. After a long drive out of London he reached their underwhelming HQ in rural Cheshunt. And there at the door to meet him was the CEO himself. 'Welcome to the world of ordinary people!' joked Sir Terry Leahy, going on to explain how HQ staff have to go and work the tills in busy stores over Christmas and New Year.

As Tesco's performance has evidenced, there are many benefits from abandoning the corner office and sitting in the trenches with your troops.

You are closer to your customers. You can eavesdrop on conversations, and get a firsthand sense of how easy or difficult things are.

Your team will mirror your behaviour if they can see you (which is fine so long as you don't sit back smoking a cigar with your feet on the table). You can stop cliques and factions forming in teams. And you can spot star performers, and slackers, without having to rely on secondhand reports.

Action points

- Have a desk in the centre of your customer support or sales team.

- If needs be, put some headphones on, or put up a notice when you are not to be disturbed.

- You can keep a back-up space to hold any more sensitive conversations.

72

Be a pacifist in the talent war

"I always invest in businesses that can be run by any idiot, because some day, they will be."

– Warren Buffett

No self-respecting business has 'employees' these days, they all have 'talent'. Apparently, in order to survive, you have to win in the 'global talent wars' to attract and retain the very best you can afford.

Actually, your business should be able to survive with the lowest possible talent for each job role.

If your company requires unique, and possibly irreplaceable, individuals to do each job, you have more than a 'talent' problem. You also don't have a business; you have a co-operative.

To grow, a business can't rely on fluke. It needs a replicable and systematic way of doing things. Anyone should be able to step into the defined places in this system. You can recruit people at a lower level and help them to grow within the business as they learn the ropes.

It doesn't mean you have to hire bland people and hammer them like cogs into your dark satanic mill. It means your business can be a proving ground for rising talent, where you train and develop the next generation of stars.

A surprising example is Barcelona Football Club. Rather than spending millions attracting star players from around the world, Barcelona relies on home-grown talent nurtured at its La Cantera football academy. Boys as young as eight join the academy, then when they are 14 they move to stay at La Masia, a converted farmhouse right next to the city's Camp Nou stadium. Barcelona, arguably the best football team in the world, aims to have 50 per cent of the team from the academy – saving them a fortune in transfer fees. The academy has produced players such as Fabregas, Iniesta and Messi.

Action points

- Look around your office. If five of the top performers were to leave this afternoon, would your company be able to survive?
- Start to document the systems that your business runs on, and make sure they can be replicated by others.
- Set up a training academy where bright new recruits can join and work their way up the business.

73
Send your team home

You want your team to be more productive? Send them home early.

If you asked most managers the best way to rate the effectiveness of their direct reports, they'll mention the results they achieve – the output. Yet look at how most employees are evaluated and you'll see it's measured on input – the hours they work and effort they make.

So you end up with a workplace where no one dares to leave early. Where overtime is seen as a badge of honour and a way of climbing the greasy pole. I've heard of companies where people buy two jackets – one to wear, and one to leave hanging over the back of their chair so their bosses think they're always in the office.

Yet a few enlightened companies are switching to 'ROWE' – a Results Only Work Environment – where employees are given complete control over the hours they work. A great example is US electrical retailer Best Buy. By switching to ROWE they found an average productivity increase of 35 per cent in departments that used it. It also increased employee retention by 27 per cent. On the flip side, the results-only system exposed underperformers, who were lazy but good at playing office politics.

Similarly, Chicago events company Red Frog give employees unlimited days off, on the stipulation that the work is always done, and cover arranged.

Action points

- Start treating your team like grown-ups. Quantify what the results are that you expect, both in terms of quantity but also quality.
- Then give people the freedom to set their own work hours around this.
- At the same time, crack down on the slackers. It can be hugely demoralising to a team to see the person who coasts get the same rewards as the grafters.

74
Don't delegate – abdicate

Very few people are natural delegators. To most managers, 'delegation' is a matter of taking a large stack of folders and dumping it on a subordinate's desk.

Real delegation is about giving someone sufficient authority to cock things up. And that responsibility is something you have to prise out of a manager's fingers like the still-smoking gun from a gunslinger's cold, dead fingers.

I speak as a terrible delegator. My worst examples are in customer meetings where a colleague is doing a presentation and I suddenly cut across them to make a correction. I might have said, 'In fact, we can deliver in three weeks,' but what the client hears is 'I don't trust my staff,' and the employee hears 'I don't pay you to have your own views.'

If you delegate properly, there is a risk of things going wrong. But if you honestly think back to your early days, you made those mistakes too. If you don't want to work yourself into an early grave, then you need to let colleagues learn the hard way and learn the valuable lessons of failure. If you're peering over their shoulder the whole time, then they'll never bother taking responsibility.

There's a simple rule of thumb – if it feels painful and scary, that's real delegation.

Action points

- From the word go, give someone total responsibility for the outcome of a project.
- Let them come and question you further, but try not to give them good advice – just query them about their decisions.
- Go on holiday.

75
Remove the safety net

I t's all very well having gung-ho gurus telling us we need to push ourselves out of envelopes and take bigger risks. But as the Western world limps from the shock of the credit crash, while we may wish to reward initiative, the last thing we want is more mavericks who risk wiping out not just themselves, but their companies and whole economies.

So now the pendulum has swung the other way. There is a growing list of checks and regulations in finance and business that try to coax the bolted horse back into the stable.

But if we genuinely want business to be safer, we need to remove the safety nets.

Many of the worst excesses of the credit crunch came about because banks thought they'd removed risk. 'We've done away with boom and bust!' crowed Gordon Brown, unaware of the growing bubble he was sat atop.

In 2001, Dutch traffic engineer Hans Monderman took a different approach. He believed that warning signs, traffic lights, railings, curbs, speed bumps and so on are not only unnecessary, but can endanger those they are meant to protect.

To test his theory, he got the denizens of the city of Drachten to remove virtually every form of traffic control, from traffic lights to lines, roundabouts and curbs from their city centre. The central traffic hub was now distinguishable only by a raised circle of grass in the middle and some pretty fountains.

A year on, his hunch was proved right. Despite an increase in traffic, congestion had decreased, and the number of accidents had halved. Monderman's favourite trick was to close his eyes and walk backwards into the centre of the busy square. The traffic parted around him and he passed through untouched.

In interviews, drivers and residents said they felt that the new square was more dangerous. Monderman was delighted; 'If they'd not felt less secure, we would have changed it immediately.' No longer seeing themselves as 'protected' by outside forces, drivers and pedestrians had to take more responsibility and care for their own safety.

Action points

- Do a risk MOT of your company.
- Make your team aware of these risks, but make it clear that the responsibility lies with them. (That's not to say you can't have a secret back-up just in case...)

REMOVE THE SAFETY NETS.

76
Sack early

I'm a fan of employment regulations. They force you to think twice about getting rid of a member of staff. Just because you've suddenly taken against a colleague, or 'their face doesn't fit', it forces you to stop being capricious and sit down to address the real problem.

But there is an exception. Despite all the processes in the world, sometimes you just make a bad hire. Even if you've had a couple of interviews, there is only so much you can glean in two short hours. And to retread the cliché, 'It's not you, it's me', chances are it is no one's fault. They're just not quite the fit you thought they'd be for the role.

In this case, you have to act decisively and ask them to quit.

The situation isn't going to magically improve, and the longer they stay, the more damage done to both of you. Your other team members also need to know they are there on merit, and not just because you are too chicken to deal with the misfits.

I once tempted a good friend to leave his secure job and work for me as a salesperson. He was a fantastic marketeer, but it turned out he just wasn't a natural cold-caller. I soon realised I'd made a hideous mistake. I'd sit skulking opposite him for weeks trying to urge him with my Jedi mind powers to pick up the phone. I finally took him out for lunch and told him it wasn't working. It was a massive relief for the both of us, and he soon went on to much bigger and better things than he would have with me.

Action points

- When recruiting, put lots of work into a job profile and make sure you've nailed not just the skills, but the attitudes and personality required.

- Set up a comprehensive induction process. Over the first few weeks, grill the recruit so you can find out if they're the right fit. And if they're not, then you need to make the call.

77
Seek out the disabled

I thought that might get your attention.

I know we're meant to feel sorry for the disabled. But if I suffered from an incapacity, I certainly wouldn't want anyone to give me work out of pity.

In business, every company needs an edge. Throughout this text I've shown how thinking and acting differently can open up great opportunities to exploit. So why not look for the unique skills that the differently-abled might provide for you?

When his son Lars was diagnosed with autism, Thorkil Sonne went into a spiral of worry. People with Autism Spectrum Disorder (ASD) typically display problems interacting with others and responding to change, which makes holding down a job difficult.

But as he watched his seven-year-old copy a complex diagram from memory, Thorkil had a flash of inspiration. In his job in IT, he knew many bugs get missed in software testing as people find it too boring. Yet people with ASD tend to show huge attention to detail and have extremely strong memories. They could be excellent in such a job.

The company he set up, Specialisterne, now employs 60 people, 45 of whom have ASD. They refuse to run as a charity, and compete head-to-head with rivals while making a strong profit from their unique difference.

Action points

- Have a think about what specialist talents and abilities might make a competitive advantage in your business.

- Forget looking for 'normal' employees, but look for the edge that comes from being special (in the real, not patronising, sense of the word).

78

Encourage trade unions

The UK's experience of union power has not been great. Through the latter half of the 20th century, many unions leveraged their collectivised muscle to extort ruinously high wage settlements or impractical working practices from cowed employers. Stories abound of the print unions in the 1970s refusing to adopt new technologies, or enforcing rigid job demarcations. Today, we have London Underground 'drivers' earning £61,000 to operate trains that largely drive themselves, and getting a £1,000 bonus just for turning up to work during the Olympics.

But it needn't be like that.

Germany's industrial might is the envy of the world, yet it has a highly collectivised approach to industrial relations. Workers have an automatic right to a seat on the representative boards of their employers. Many industries outsource collective bargaining to agree set wages for workers across the industry. And yet this approach led to workers agreeing to keep down their wages rates and so maintain a competitive advantage while labour costs soared in other European countries from Greece to France.

One of the secrets of Germany's success comes from uniting organisations behind a common goal that often transcends narrow or short-term individual objectives. They set out a vision of how all members of society will benefit from the success of an enterprise.

It also requires managers to exercise restraint in their own rewards. As one German MD said, 'It's important as owners that we're not greedy and are willing to leave more on the table.' Compared to our 'winner takes all' manifesto that seemingly obliges each individual to maximise their personal winnings, it's not surprising how adversarial our society has become.

Action points

- Define and articulate a common purpose in your business that stretches beyond your short-term interests.

- Once everyone's interests are aligned, allow your team to agree how they will share in this success.

- Exercise restraint.

79
Fire the founder

Entrepreneurs are amazing people. They can conjure opportunity out of seemingly thin air, and bring uncommon tenacity to hunt it to the ground in the face of all obstacles.

But they have their time and place.

For a start, you only want one in any business. Two mavericks trying to head in opposite directions will tear a business apart. You need clarity, and staff need to know who to answer to. You also want to keep them locked in the asylum; the bloody-mindedness that drives sales can wreak havoc when let loose on employee relations.

They're also valuable for a specific phase in a company's development. When you've moved from the battleground of market proving to the sunny uplands where success is based on nurturing clients and sustained profit, their skills possibly aren't so valuable.

Venture Capital firms are notorious for their lack of sentimentality when it comes to such decisions. Of the *Wall Street Journal*'s top VC-backed companies in 2010, less than half still had their founder in charge.

But what of Steve Jobs, I hear you cry? He was renowned for having the most successful second act in history. But that's the definition of a second act. In his first act, Apple was running aground at speed. It was only after taking a career break that Jobs was able to 're-start' the company in a new way.

Action points

- There will be many elements of your business that do not need 'an entrepreneur's touch'. Keep the founder away from them.

- If you are the founder, consider when it's time to quit. Take a sabbatical, or go and launch a new product.

- You need balance in an organisation, but that doesn't mean you only need to employ balanced people. Just ensure the system is there to channel them.

80
Cultivate some enemies

'No one likes us, we don't care!' rang the famous Millwall Football Club chant in the 1970s. And as I explained to my tearful daughter, there is nothing that unites a group in the playground more than letting someone know they are not allowed in the gang.

Indeed, the lack of a common enemy can be ruinous to a group's cohesion. The Salem Witch Trials are seen by some as a group tearing itself apart looking for a new enemy to unite against, as they had done when they battled to first establish their community in the face of religious persecution.

In business, you're better off being pirates than the navy. You just need to identify who you are up against.

Scottish brewers BrewDog live by this credo. Set up by James Watt and Martin Dickie to take on 'the faceless, generic, monolithic, multinational corporations who make pathetic, fizzy, yellow, insipid cardboard', they have embraced a piratical approach at every turn. Lambasted by regulators for selling strong beer, they responded by releasing a 1.1 per cent 'Nanny State' beer. When a German brewery topped their strongest beer, BrewDog produced a 41 per cent proof 'Sink the Bismarck' beer. They also launched 'the world's smallest protest'– a dwarf carrying a placard in an attempt to change the law to allow beer to be served in two-thirds of a pint. They won.

But it runs deeper than marketing hype. To raise money for a new brewery, they ignored their advisors and turned to customers. Through the 'Equity for Punks' scheme, they raised £2.1 million in new finance, and recruited a new flotilla of fellow pirates.

Action points

- Identify who the 'navy' is in your industry. Even better if they are a larger organisation and a smug conglomerate.

- If you realise with horror that you are the navy, then set up a secret pirate team that can really get things done, then gradually subvert your company from the inside out.

Part six
Finance

81

Pay yourself
£1,000 an hour

As you grow a business, it's understandable you'd want to keep yourself cheap and affordable. It's the same if you're an employee; you don't want to price yourself out of the market, or be seen as a 'fat cat' creaming the money that others richly deserve.

It's a laudable view, but misguided. If you undervalue yourself, you'll never grow your business. You need to work out what your true value is.

The most important cost in your business is your 'opportunity cost'. This term was first coined by economist Friedrich von Wieser in 1914, who defined it as 'the true cost of an activity measured in terms of the value of the next best alternative forgone'.

In practical terms, do you think that spending an hour delivering the order to your customer will save you £40 in courier fees? Not if you could have spent that hour doing sales calls that could bring in £4,000. In trying to save £40, you've actually lost £3,960.

Action points

- There's a simple exercise to work out what your true hourly rate should be.

  1. Work out how much you want to grow your business by this year.

  2. Divide this figure by 1,740 (the average number of hours we work each year).

  3. That's your hourly 'opportunity cost'.

- Now look at every task you do in your business. Anything you do that is worth less than that figure, you should delegate or pay someone else to do. It may seem like a cost in the short term, but it's the only way that you'll grow.

- There's a kicker. You don't actually have to pay yourself that amount. But you do need to know what it is. And if you don't take it seriously, don't scratch your head in years to come when you wonder why you're still just packing crates.

82
Max out your credit cards

Y ou've got a brilliant new business idea. You lock yourself in a room fine-tuning your business plan and
then hit the road pitching to angel investors and venture capitalists to raise the big bucks you need to launch it.

Take this advice from Mark McCormack, author of *What
They Don't Teach you at Harvard Business School*: 'The
more up-front money a business requires, the less chance it
has of getting off the ground.'

Instead, launch your idea by maxing out some credit cards.

Your banker and your friends will probably tell you this is
a terrible source of start-up cash. Shouldn't you put in place
more sustainable, long-term and cheaper finance to properly fund your growth?

True, but it neglects the vital fact that what you need
most in a start-up is space and time to get things wrong.
It's time in which you watch your customers and find out
what they *really* want from your product or service. With
too much cash, chances are you'll blow it on a flash bit of
kit that subsequently turns out to be totally wrong for your
business. Too late!

A year after registering Google.com, Sergey Brin and Larry Page had about 10,000 people using the site, but they didn't have sufficient computer storage to provide a fast enough service. They'd spotted a good deal on bulk hard drives but were low on cash. Rather than hit the funding trail, they maxed their credit cards, their friends' cards, and their parents' resources until they had enough cash to buy 120 hard drives. A year later, Google was answering 500,000 searches a day, and Brin and Page could secure $25 million of funding at much better terms. In 2010 they made a profit of $29.3 billion.

Action points

- Start cheap. If you've got a good idea, use your credit cards if you need to; just buy yourself the time to test things out.

- Once you've proved it works, and won a strong stream of orders, then consider going cap in hand to funders to ramp it up.

83
Don't lend £10,000 to your brother

I love my brothers (I have three), and my sister. They spoilt me as a child, and I know they'd be there for me. I'd give them a kidney, but I'd think twice about lending them ten grand.

Yet every day, businesspeople lend sums way in excess of this to complete strangers.

I remember in my first publishing business, I turned up at the printers with a briefcase full of cash I'd begged, cajoled and threatened out of my customers. The printer said, 'That's OK, you don't have to pay us for another month.' I was staggered, and very nearly fell into the nearest pub to celebrate with my briefcase.

It never ceases to amaze me how people give new customers generous payment terms of a month or more, and then fail to chase up payment, just because it's 'what you do'.

I'm not pretending you can expect every customer to pay cash on delivery. Just don't get into the lazy habit of doling out credit automatically. Negotiate as hard with your payment terms as you do with your price. Only give credit where it's due, the customer has earned it, or paid extra for it.

If you want a master class, try selling something to a professional Indian buyer. As one said to me with pride, 'We know how to hold our suppliers' feet to the fire!' They'll use every technique to get a good deal, such as benchmarking all your input costs, using silence as a negotiating technique, or feigning rudeness. And when you've 'got a deal', you'll have to negotiate just as hard to get payment.

Action points

- Ditch any 'standard payment terms' from your price list and invoices.
- Don't automatically give credit to new customers unless it's essential to closing the deal.
- Negotiate each case as it comes, and only give credit once they've proved themselves.

I LOVE MY

BROTHERS

(I HAVE THREE),

AND MY SISTER.

I'D GIVE THEM A

KIDNEY,

BUT I'D THINK

TWICE ABOUT

LENDING THEM

TEN GRAND.

84
Be unaffordable

I found myself chuckling with glee recently as I loaded up my supermarket trolley with an unbelievable £2 chicken offer. But as I wandered around the store, I began to worry. What kind of life must that chicken have lived? What corners had they cut to price a chicken at £2? And I was about to serve it to my kids. They'd probably sprout a pair of breasts.

Price isn't just about affordability. It's an incredibly powerful signal of many subconscious values.

A great example is 'Veblen goods'. Named after Thorstein Veblen, a US economist and social scientist who, in 1899, coined the term 'conspicuous consumption', these are commodities such as perfume and watches that become more desirable the more expensive they are.

'What suckers!' you might think. But Veblen's hunch has recently found support by advances in MRI brain-imaging. Researchers at the California Institute of Technology ran brain scans on people drinking an identical glass of wine. However, when subjects were told the wine cost $45 compared to $5 a glass, the part of the brain that registers pleasure lit up more actively. Their actual experience of pleasure was heightened by the subconscious cues their brains were receiving.

Price is a powerful signal. French brandy exporters discovered this in China, where social status is hugely important. People wear their work name badges at weekends to show they have an office job, or leave the labels on the outsides of their suits. Luxury items are valued often not just for their innate value, but for the messages they send out. So when selling their brandy, retailers will deliberately leave a bottle on the top shelf that is always priced out of reach – whatever price the customer offers.

Action points

- Have you thought what signals your prices send out about your business?

- While you don't have to move into the luxury bracket, offering a few prestige items at unaffordable prices can send out a valuable message to customers about the quality of your offering.

85
Don't compensate for the size of your manhood

'When you're sitting on top of the mountain, it's amazing how many people want to help you out,' said a successful entrepreneur to me, 'but I saw no sight of them in the long years I was pushing the boulder up the bloody long hill!'

Growing a business organically can be a long, painful slog. How tempting then to short cut this graft and grow by acquisition. In buying a competitor, you'll vault your industry peers in a single move, and arrive in the big league.

Before you start envisaging the applause and decking out your new corner office, take a look at the stats:

- 83 per cent of mergers studied were unsuccessful in producing any business benefits regarding shareholder value (KPMG, 1999).

- A study of 150 major deals led *Business Week* to conclude that half actually destroyed shareholder value.

- In the first eight months following a deal, productivity in both companies is typically reduced by up to 50 per cent (Huang & Kleiner, 2004).

Too often, acquisitions are driven by bloodlust, ego and possibly compensation activity, rather than cold logic. Purchases are consistently made at the wrong price, at the wrong time, and for the wrong reasons. For the brave, there are opportunities to buy in times of adversity ('The time to buy is when there's blood on the streets,' as Warren Buffett remarks). But for most of the time, it's about ego.

Action points

- If you're thinking of buying rather than building, check your motives. Better yet, get a devil's advocate to quiz you about it.
- Discount your assumptions like crazy. When calculating the price, factor in the cost of a 50 per cent drop in production, and 40 per cent of customers and staff heading for the door. Is it still worth doing?
- Hire more salespeople instead.

86

Say 'no' to cheap money

S itting opposite a banker, and negotiating a loan, you are going to want the lowest figure possible, and will be prepared to walk if you don't get it.

But a flood of 'cheap money' in the form of debt or equity can be more damaging to your business than crack cocaine. And just as addictive.

We've just been through one of history's greatest financial crises. Many people would be happy to revisit a parliamentary resolution that followed the 'South Sea Bubble' of 1720 which proposed bankers be tied in sacks filled with snakes and thrown in the Thames.

But I believe the consumers of this debt bear an equal share of the blame. The flood of cheap money from Chinese savers pushed loan rates to artificially low levels and pushed consumers into becoming debt junkies.

My favourite example is Hollywood mogul Harvey Weinstein. Having built a reputation for producing gold-plated hits, he found himself armed with a war chest of £1 billion from generous bankers. His first acquisition in 2006 was a Facebook rival for the mega-rich, then he bought a cable network, followed by a fashion house. The normal disciplines he'd honed in straightened times went out the window. And just as quickly as his new empire went up, it all came crashing down. He's back to what he does best, making films.

Action points

- Creative thinking comes in constrained circumstances. Indulge in the money drug, and that goes out the window.
- Only look for debt when you have a clear business opportunity you can tap into fast, and are crystal clear on your repayment terms.
- If the pushers come knocking – just say 'no'.

87

Double your costs, halve your reward

I f you've produced a business plan (and ignored Rule 19), I hope you are doing it to raise finance. Chances are you've put in a realistic set of figures.

That's fine for your funders, but now you need to double your costs and halve your revenues.

By nature, entrepreneurs and pioneers are optimists. That's fine in setting goals and targets. But your financial projections are not the place to play ego games. When it comes to financial planning, it's the time to think like a depressed Scottish farmer caught in a downpour. Add 40 per cent to your overheads. See those 'rock solid' orders? Scratch a couple of them. How do the figures stack up now?

As a wise man said, 'Expect the best, but prepare for the worst.' The most depressing business stories I hear are of promising businesses that go bust through 'over-trading'. They've got a great pipeline of orders, but for the want of the smallest amount of working cash, they go bust.

However sophisticated your financial modelling, you simply cannot predict the future, so you need a bit of 'wobble room'.

Follow the example of Scottish oil explorer Bill Gammell at Cairn Energy. I interviewed him about their approach to risk. He explained their modelling, their geologists' work, the scenario planning, but at the end of the planning process he would take whatever figures his technical team gave him, double the risk, and halve the rewards. If it still stacked up, then they would go for it.

Action point

- Don't put vanity assumptions into your business plan. Make sure it's viable at even the most pessimistic levels. Then allow your spending to rise with actual income.

88

Set fire to your price list

There's a sensible way to set your prices. You take all your input costs and staff time, then add an industry-standard margin, and end up with a simple and clear price list.

You might as well build a bonfire of cash outside your office and set fire to it.

Your costs only tell you one thing – if you've negotiated a good price from your suppliers. Your price is completely different. It's what your customers are willing to pay on any given day, in any given place, for any given reason. You'd be better off using a psychologist to set your price list rather than an accountant.

There are all kinds of factors you can use to vary the price of what you sell.

Take the example of hardback books. When publishing yearbooks, I found that by adding a £2 hard binding, I could charge £7 more per book – and customers were happier with the prestige of a hardback. But that's nothing to 'airport exclusives' of books. By using the fig leaf of a slightly larger page size, publishers can charge 40 per cent more just to capitalise on customers' lack of patience.

Snob value is an obvious pricing strategy, or you can vary your price list based on urgency. A consultant was working with a business that helped companies put out fires. They had a standard hourly price list, until the consultant pointed out how much a fire in an oil well would cost a company compared to, say, a warehouse blaze.

Action points

- You need a price list with variations. You need to flex it depending on factors such as snob value, urgency, time of day, customer use or context.
- Get your best salespeople involved in deciding what price you can command. Then hand the list to your finance department and see if they can negotiate costs to deliver an acceptable margin at these price points.

89

Treat suppliers like fellow combatants

When tough times hit, it's natural to want to pass on the pain to your suppliers. You'll want to squeeze them until the pips squeak in pursuit of a good price.

But this can do more harm than good.

Your suppliers can become one of the best ways to get yourself out of a tight corner. As Darrell Rigby of consultants Bain and Co. points out, smart companies 'treat their suppliers as fellow combatants trapped in the same foxhole'.

Rigby cited the example of Chrysler. In the teeth of the 1990 recession, the car giant had to realise significant savings. But rather than simply offload the pain onto their suppliers, Chrysler embraced them. They outsourced more of their operations to suppliers, which helped them cut inventory. Then they announced that if any supplier could come up with a way to save more than 10 per cent of a cost, Chrysler would split the savings with them.

Chrysler used the money to invest in new models and was the only one of the big US car makers to turn a profit the following year.

Action points

- If you're hit by a downturn, visit your core suppliers and share the problem with them.

- Incentivise suppliers by offering to share savings if they can identify significant cost reductions, or ways you can both work more profitably together.

- Work out the long-term benefits from outsourcing more of what you do to suppliers.

Part seven
Personal

90

Cry as a negotiating technique

When a mistake happens, you switch into damage limitation mode. It's only natural to want to immediately stem any possible repercussions and liabilities from your customers.

The problem is that customers can spot this dash for cover a mile off. The more you try to hide the damage, the more they'll pursue you. If you are not careful, their fuelled sense of outrage can spread like wildfire to other customers.

The best piece of business advice I got when starting up came from a grizzled entrepreneur who said, 'Learn crying as a negotiation technique.'

The moment you spot a mistake, confess. Resist the urge to duck and dive. Phone up your customer and apologise sincerely. Better yet, turn up in person, and lay yourself prostrate at their feet and beg their forgiveness.

I started out publishing university yearbooks. Working late one night, I didn't notice how Microsoft Word, in its infinite wisdom, had decided to 'correct' the name of the class president by taking the 'G' out of Angus McDonald.

I only spotted the blunder on the morning of delivery. So I took the books to the customer and told them immediately.

I apologised profusely and offered a number of solutions to rectify the solution. After a startled pause, they burst out laughing. It seemed it was an apt description of Angus. A couple of beers later and it became a treasured item.

The truth is that a fast, clear and unequivocal apology is utterly disarming. There's nothing for a customer to push up against, and their sense of injustice is immediately deflated. And customers who've been through a successfully resolved problem tend to be more loyal in the longer term.

Action points

- Don't foster a culture of blame in your organisation. When a mistake occurs, there's no benefit in instituting a witch-hunt, and it'll cause lasting damage.

- The moment you spot a serious mistake, take the initiative. Be fulsome and heartfelt in your apology, and start to outline the remedies you will take. The slightest whiff that you are trying to shift the blame, and the customer will come after you.

- It doesn't mean you have to go overboard. With a strong apology, offer them a practical and proportionate fix to the problem.

91
Pile on the stress

We have recently seen a march of CEOs vacate the top seat citing stress. When Antonio Horta-Osario took a leave of absence from Lloyds, he revealed his 'torture' at not having slept for five days straight.

It certainly adds to the picture of the loneliness of the CEO. Who would want to climb that high and pay such a price?

In fact, research shows that stress actually decreases with promotion.

From the 1960s on, the 'Whitehall Studies' have taken a long look at the working habits of civil servants. Early in the study, researchers found that those lower in the pecking order, such as messengers and door-keepers, had *twice* the rate of heart attacks than those further up, even after controlling for other external factors. And the higher you rise, the healthier you become.

This isn't just medicine for mandarins. The studies have been repeated around the world and revealed the exact same trend. Stress-related illnesses tend to decrease as you get promoted.

There is debate over the causes. I believe a large factor is the importance of control over your destiny. In a lowly position, stress happens to you, and this releases the stress hormone cortisol. Normally you'd choose a 'fight or flight' response but there are fewer options available to you and the cortisol remains sluicing around your system. When you have the handbrake applied but your foot flat on the accelerator, it's no surprise your oil pressure starts to head towards exploding point.

Other studies in Finland suggest a lack of 'predictability' in lower grade jobs leads to increased stress, and other researchers have shown a correlation between health and self-esteem in troops of monkeys.

Whatever the reasons, the studies are clear. If you want to walk the longer path, then be prepared to shoulder a heavier burden.

Action point

● Don't let the fear of stress hold you back from seeking advancement.

92
Avoid the passion trap

A couple of winters ago on my walk home from work, I noticed a shiny new Cocktail Emporium that had sprung up. Inside stood a very proud storekeeper, surrounded by his exotic elixirs in an otherwise empty store. I asked around and found he was a senior director at a global financial company who'd taken early redundancy and ploughed the money into his life's passion – cocktails.

As the bitter winter marched on, the store's lights burned bright, the storekeeper busied himself around his empty store in his bright white apron, but the smile was sliding by slow notches. And then one evening, the lights were off. Then the 'For Sale' boards went up.

'To succeed in business, you must follow your life's passion,' suggests the homily. If we throw our hearts into doing what we truly love, then success will surely follow.

Unfortunately, there's a world of difference between doing what you love, and making money from doing what you love. Doing one can kill the other.

For a start, you have to carefully ration how long you spend on the pleasurable bit so you can make a profit. You then have to sell your precious creation to a philistine audience who don't appreciate it the way you do. And then the buggers don't pay you for it so you have to chase them!

Repeat this process, day after day, possibly outsourcing the creative bit you love so you can focus on flogging it, and you can see the one way to kill a passion is having to make a living from it.

We spend too much of our lives working not to do what we enjoy or are brilliant at. But before you're tempted to tell your boss where to shove his memo and stride out the door to follow your dreams, think a bit harder about the *process* of making a living from doing what you love. Do you yearn to be more creative? Do you like working in a team? Do you mind selling? By thinking rationally about the process, and then building your life around this, the chances are you can enjoy work and your life.

Action point

- Hate your boss? Feeling unappreciated in your job? Keen to try something different? That's not enough of a reason to start up on your own. That's a reason to get a better job.

93
Don't give money to charity

You've reached a plateau of success. In sober moments of reflection you acknowledge that your achievements were not solely down to your innate talent, charm and good looks. You've been lucky to benefit from the actions of others, your friends and parents, and, sometimes, divine providence. It's time to give something back.

I'm a huge admirer of faiths like Islam that require adherents to give a set percentage of their annual income to charity. However I think money is too cheap a way of paying those debts. Bunging £100 to a charity auction doesn't get you off the hook, I'm afraid.

Reports by a range of charities such as Care International suggest that money raised to respond to natural disasters often leaves the afflicted worse-off than before. They want people to give to sustainable causes and for prevention, but these rarely make the headlines.

The most valuable thing you can give is of yourself. What unique skill or talent has taken you to the position of fortune? You should donate a proportion of that.

The best example of this is 'Billanthropy' as practised by Bill Gates. To back up his massive financial commitment, Gates deploys his skills and those of his company to develop technical solutions, implementation and project management in the fight to eradicate malaria.

Action points

- Work out what your unique talent or strength is.
- Find an organisation that means something to you.
- Marry the two – try to think how you can leverage that skill to help in pursuit of a defined goal that motivates you. Don't think that just because you want to help, chucking money at the problem is enough.

94
Stop thinking positive

Ever since *The Power of Positive Thinking* by Norman Vincent Peale hit the bookshelves in 1952, we've been swamped by self-help books. Not only does 'positive thinking' not work, it's actively detrimental.

There is a self-fulfilling truth that people who believe themselves to be lucky genuinely are. Researchers tested this by putting an advert in a newspaper saying, 'If you spot this, claim your reward!' Of the test subjects who read the paper, only those who'd rated themselves as 'lucky' claimed their reward.

The problem, as experimenters have found, is that forcing people with low self-esteem to try to think positively actually made them feel worse.

If I said to you, 'For the next 20 minutes, don't think about Polar bears,' guess what's going to keep popping into your head (and why on *earth* is he riding a unicycle?). In the same way, a study told two groups to think of their worst personal experiences, then one group were told not to think of these for the rest of the week. Of course, they thought about them more, and ended up feeling more depressed and with lower self-esteem.

And visualisation (and 'cosmic ordering') causes similar problems. Researchers Heather Kappes and Gabriele Oettingen, writing in the *Journal of Experimental Social Psychology,* found the problem is that when you visualise, the brain takes the bait. Measuring the blood pressure and brain activity of subjects asked to visualise success, the brain and body react as if the subject has already got there, and then relaxes. The result is that you end up with less energy and brain power to actually get you to your nirvana.

Ironically, the one thing visualisation is good for is managing anxiety. If you want to calm down, and put less pressure on reaching targets, then visualise them.

Action points

- A positive attitude is vital in business, but you can't force it.
- Instead, invest in time spent doing things that motivate you, and then try and carry that positive buzz into your work.

95
Disinherit your kids

"Shrouds have no pockets."

– Old Scottish proverb

If you've worked hard to build something up, it's only natural you'll want to preserve this and pass it on to your nearest and dearest. It's as if we're trying to deny the fact that our presence on earth is anything more than footsteps on a sandy beach.

On one hand, holding on is the enemy of creativity. The moment you start trying to nail things down, they become illusive. Being possessive makes you stagnate and stops ideas from flowing. In the words of Ian Brown, singer with (reformed) The Stone Roses, 'Keep what you've got by giving it all away'.

But if that's too airy-fairy, then its worth bearing in mind that making life easy for your progeny is possibly the least useful thing you can do for them. Rather than passing on your wealth, why not pass on the drive and hunger that created that money in the first place?

A growing group of American billionaires has signed up to the 'Giving Pledge' to acknowledge this. Following Warren Buffett's dictum on inheritance that he wants to give his children 'enough that they can do anything, but not so much that they do nothing', they're committed to giving away the majority of their wealth.

Action points

- If you want to pass on something, then consider giving your successors a degree of freedom.
- Buy them a round-the-world air ticket, pay off student debts, give them funds to travel. But that's it. Make it crystal clear that after that, they're on their own.

96
Nurture self-doubt

"If you believe you can, you can.
If you believe you can't, you're right."

– Henry Ford

A cast-iron sense of self-belief is a valuable ally in building a business. It'll help you through the dark hours before dawn when all available evidence seems to point to you being a bone-headed numpty.

But over time, it can become a great hindrance. You start to believe the reports of your personal infallibility.

A number of experiments have demonstrated the effect of 'confirmation bias'. This is a tendency to view neutral findings as supporting your particular set of beliefs (researchers are not immune, setting up experiments that are biased from the start).

This is then backed by 'communal reinforcement'. Nobel laureate Daniel Kahneman summarises this in his book, *Thinking, Fast and Slow*: 'We know that people can maintain an unshakeable faith in any proposition, however absurd, when they are sustained by a community of like-minded believers.' Cult leaders have long recognised this.

This heady cocktail of delusion is then topped off with 'primacy effect', where people form a stronger attachment to evidence they received early in an experiment.

And what happens when you shake up this devil's brew? RBS happens.

The bank was riding high from an earlier successful take-over of NatWest. It was helmed by a chief executive with a pretty robust view of his self-worth, commanding a tight-knit management clique with a low tolerance of dissenting opinion. They were masterfully played by the Dutch owners of ABN Amro, leaving them hanging around in airports, into paying massively over the odds for their bank. It ended up with UK taxpayers having to bail out RBS to the tune of £45 billion.

Action points

- Heed the advice of Rudyard Kipling: 'Treat success and failure as the twin imposters they are.'
- Hire a 'court jester' – someone who is licensed to tell you the truth, however inconvenient or uncomfortable that might be (family members are usually quite good for this!).

97
Jump off a chair

Looking at daredevil entrepreneurs who divide their time between running global enterprises and parachuting out of spaceships, you'd think the world is divided into superheroes and the rest of us. These amazing individuals seemingly leapt out of their mothers' wombs on bungee cords.

I'm not convinced. I don't want to wade knee-deep into the debate as to whether entrepreneurs (or indeed any other personality types) are born or made. I do believe some people are born with a head start, and I also agree you can't take a group of 12-year-olds and turn all of them into go-getting tycoons. But you can teach people to have a higher tolerance for risk and uncertainty.

When younger, I learnt to parachute with the army. The motto of the training wing is 'Knowledge dispels fear'. Rather than shouting at you and bundling you out of a plane, they build you up. You start by doing a lot of falling over. Then you jump off benches and chairs, then walls. You graduate up to a tower and harness until after much preparation, you gleefully throw yourself out the back of a C130 transport plane.

It's the same in business. Most of the people who sit at the top of billion-dollar enterprises built their way up in small steps. I was also taken with the biography of Richard

Branson, whose mother was forever devising independence
and confidence tests for him as he grew up.

Action points

- If you want your team to grow in confidence, then
  deliberately set out a series of confidence-building steps.
  These can be the size of projects, or conquering a fear
  like presenting to senior clients. They'll find that most
  of our fears live most potently in our own imaginations,
  and dissipate when exposed to daylight.

- The same rule applies to children. Step back. If you're
  always there to stop them from falling, they'll never
  learn how to pick themselves up again.

98
Be a psychopath

Do you have a psychopath for a boss?

There are a number of excellent articles and books, such as Jon Ronson's *The Psychopath Test*, highlighting the similarity between psychopaths and some chief executives. It makes a nice story, particularly for anyone who's suffered under an overweening boss. It also seems to have some research basis.

Psychologists at Surrey University recently found out that three of 11 personality disorders were actually more common in high-level executives than in inmates of Broadmoor Hospital. Traits like narcissism, obsessive compulsion and histrionic disorder helped propel people up the ranks of their professions.

While I'm not advocating walking around in your mother's wedding dress, or taking glee from the suffering of others, there is one trait that is extremely useful in business. In broad terms, psychopaths are less concerned about the opinions of wider society in the course of their actions.

To be successful, you often need to walk out of step with the rest of the world. To do this it helps if you don't care too much about how others perceive you. It's surprisingly hard to do, as social scientists posit that we take at least half our sense of self-identity from the opinions of others.

A great exponent of this art is Felix Dennis, founder of Dennis Publishing. An iconoclast from his schooldays, Dennis has maintained a healthy disregard for the strictures of others. When a publishing entrepreneur came to him with the idea of a weekly news-sheet, his board blocked the idea. Dennis went behind their backs and did the deal regardless. The resulting newspaper, *The Week,* rapidly grew to become the most successful title the company ever published.

Action points

- Stop going to industry events (unless you do so in disguise). The more prominent you become in your industry, the harder it will be for you to do something genuinely innovative.

- Be aware of who your 'hidden assassins' are. Think of a new idea, and then run through in your mind who you'd be most worried about telling it to. And then – don't tell them!

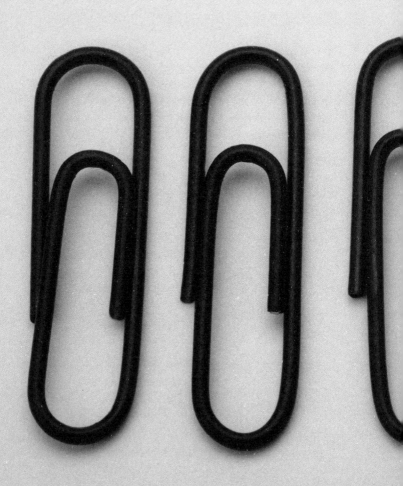

WALK OUT OF STEP WITH THE

REST OF THE WORLD.

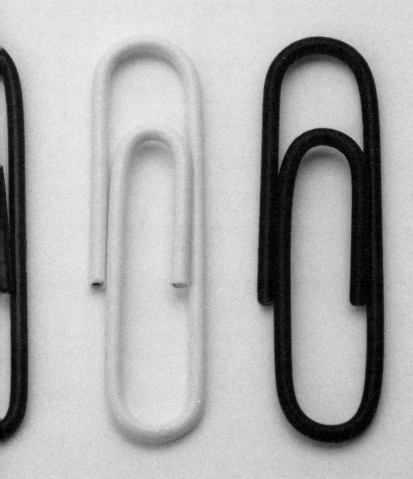

99
Don't get harpooned

I t's immensely flattering to be quoted in the media. Even better if you are spotted in the street. It validates your sense of self-worth and boosts your social status.

But before you take on a personal PR, heed the advice that Dennis Thatcher gave to Sarah Ferguson, Duchess of York (which she resolutely ignored): 'Whales only get harpooned when they spout.'

You need to be aware of the agenda of the media. It is not always to communicate the 'truth'. More often, the primary objective is to simply sell more media. And the stuff that sells media is often not the reasoned messages you want to get across.

You might make a name for yourself initially. But pretty soon, you're yesterday's news. And then the media will need a new angle on you to make you news again.

'Our firm's earrings are cheaper than a prawn cocktail sandwich, and unlikely to last as long!' quipped Gerald Ratner to an amused Institute of Directors conference in 1991. In two minutes of grandstanding, he wiped £500 million from the value of Ratners jewellers.

Action points

- PR can be a very cost-effective way to build your business, but before you return that journalist's call, think:
  - What is the message I want to get across, and how will this financially benefit my business?
  - What is the risk here, and is there a safer way to achieve the same financial benefit?
  - Do I know a professional who can help me to manage this?

100
Be lazy

'Sonny-boy, the only place achievement comes before effort is in the dictionary.' The grizzled veteran looked down at me with his hand on my shoulder.

It's a fiercely competitive world out there, and if you want to make it big, you've got to work crazy hours. I've heard of city-boys in their twenties getting Botox injections so the evidence of their 20-hour work shifts can't be seen in pitches.

That's nothing compared to emerging economies. 'Sister Dong' is the legendary leader of Gree, a Chinese manufacturing giant. She's reported not to have taken a single day off in 20 years. When she saw her young son after a ten-year hiatus, she reputedly made him catch the bus back to the airport at the end of the day.

But the world is also full of busy fools. It's easy to mistake activity for achievement. Working long hours gives people the impression of being useful. It takes much more resolution and strength sometimes to do nothing, to let things develop, to sit back and not leap into frenzied activity. As the saying goes, 'Show a lazy man a hard job and he'll find an easy way to do it.'

Looking at a table of working hours compiled by the OECD, guess which nation worked the second longest hours (after South Korea)? Greece. And Germany is way down the list with some of the shortest working hours in Europe.

There are seasons in business when fast and intense activity is essential. But at all other times, you should think like the lion basking in the shade of the African tree.

Action points

- Try never to do the same job in the same way twice. Always be looking for ways to find short cuts or delegate tasks.
- Don't worry about not being 'busy enough'. If you give yourself freedom, you'll be able to concentrate on the really important things.
- Subscribe to the Ferris Bueller theory of life: 'Life moves pretty fast. If you don't stop and look around once in a while, you could miss it.'

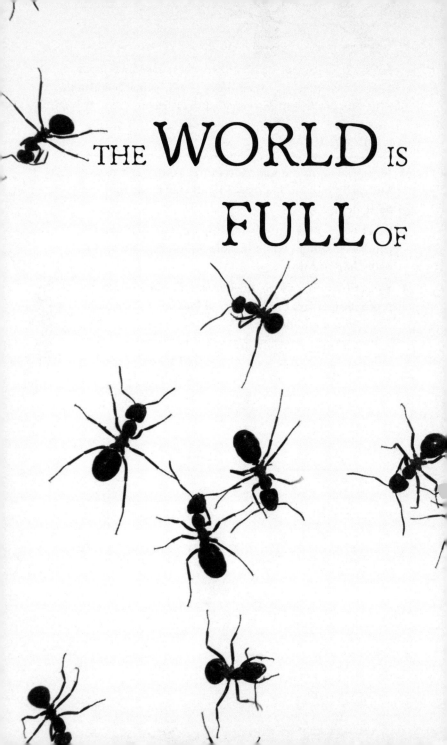

THE WORLD IS FULL OF

BUSY FOOLS.